Anonymus

Return of judicial rents fixed by Sub-Commissions and Civil Bill Courts

Notified to Irish Land Commission, March and April 1892

Anonymus

Return of judicial rents fixed by Sub-Commissions and Civil Bill Courts
Notified to Irish Land Commission, March and April 1892

ISBN/EAN: 9783742810328

Manufactured in Europe, USA, Canada, Australia, Japa

Cover: Foto ©Andreas Hilbeck / pixelio.de

Manufactured and distributed by brebook publishing software
(www.brebook.com)

Anonymus

Return of judicial rents fixed by Sub-Commissions and Civil Bill Courts

Irish Land Commission.

The Land Law (Ireland) Act, 1881, 44 & 45 Victoria, ch. 49

The Land Law (Ireland) Act, 1887, 50 & 51 Victoria, ch. 33.

RETURN

ACCORDING TO PROVINCES AND COUNTIES

OF

JUDICIAL RENTS

FIXED BY

CHIEF COMMISSION,

SUB-COMMISSIONS,

AND

CIVIL BILL COURTS,

AS NOTIFIED TO THE IRISH LAND COMMISSION DURING THE MONTHS OF

MARCH AND APRIL, 1892,

SPECIFYING DATES AND AMOUNTS RESPECTIVELY OF THE LAST INCREASES
OF RENT WHERE ASCERTAINED;

ALSO

RENTS FIXED UPON THE REPORTS OF VALUERS APPOINTED BY THE IRISH LAND
COMMISSION ON THE JOINT APPLICATIONS OF LANDLORDS AND TENANTS.

Presented to both Houses of Parliament by Command of Her Majesty.

DUBLIN:

PRINTED FOR HER MAJESTY'S STATIONERY OFFICE,

BY ALEXANDER THOM & CO. (LIMITED).

And to be purchased, either directly or through any Bookseller, from
HODGES, FIGGIS, and Co., 104, Grafton-street, Dublin; or
EYRE and SPOTTISWOODE, East Harding-street, Fleet-street, E.C.; or
JOHN MENZIES and Co. 12, Hanover-street, Edinburgh, and 90, West Nile-street, Glasgow.

INDEX.

MARCH, 1892.

SUMMARIES FOR MARCH, 1892.

Summary showing, according to Provinces and Counties, the Number of Cases in which Judicial Rents have been Fixed by Chief Commission and Sub-Commissions, under the Land Law (Ireland) Act, 1881, during the Month of March, 1892; and the Acreage, Tenement Valuations, Former Rents, and Judicial Rents of the Holdings.

Province and County.	Number of Cases in which Judicial Rents have been fixed.	Acreage.			Tenement Valuation.			Former Rent.			Judicial Rent.		
		Statute Acres			£	s.	d.	£	s.	d.	£	s.	d.
		A.	R.	P.									
ULSTER—													
Antrim	17	841	3	27	237	15	0	253	0	5½	200	0	0
Donegal	8	178	1	29	125	16	0	126	15	10	94	0	0
Fermanagh	8	63	0	11	27	10	0	23	5	10	18	18	5
Tyrone	21	763	0	22	275	14	0	312	11	0	241	14	5
Total	54	1,853	1	2	662	3	0	715	17	7¼	568	3	0
LEINSTER—													
Kildare	1	9	1	53	8	13	0	7	12	0	5	15	0
Kilkenny	1	19	0	6	18	10	0	14	4	0	14	4	8
King's	26	728	1	3	337	17	0	430	0	7	352	9	10
Meath	7	412	2	10	454	0	0	308	17	4	184	11	4
Wexford	8	227	3	57	71	0	0	133	12	8	102	9	0
Total	43	1,397	0	7	880	0	0	1,103	14	7	929	3	8
CONNAUGHT—													
Galway	35	881	2	11	229	18	0	109	13	1	338	11	4
Leitrim	20	475	3	1	110	7	0	141	4	0	110	8	8
Roscommon	64	1,815	7	25	434	10	0	565	15	8	409	15	2
Total	119	3,172	0	7	874	15	5	1,117	13	8	804	19	8

IRELAND.

CIVIL BILL COURTS.

SUMMARY FOR MARCH, 1892.

Cases in which Judicial Rents have been fixed by Civil Bill Courts under the Land Law (Ireland) Act, 1881, and notified to the Irish Land Commission during the Month of March, 1892.

Province and County.	Number of Cases in which Judicial Rents have been fixed.	Acreage.	Tenement Valuation.	Former Rent.	Judicial Rent.
		Statute Acres. A. R. P.	£ s. d.	£ s. d.	£ s. d.
ULSTER—					
Londonderry, —	1	1 0 33	surrendered,	5 1 0	2 10 0
LEINSTER					
Carlow, —	4	117 3 17	73 0 0	100 16 0	62 10 8
CONNAUGHT—					
Leitrim, —	5	53 2 19	17 15 0	19 7 6	13 0 0
MUNSTER—					
Cork, —	1	116 0 0	51 0 0	70 0 0	19 0 0
Kerry, —	19	765 2 39	220 10 6	368 18 1	279 17 6
Limerick, —	16	507 3 37	411 0 0	625 19 8	433 15 0
Total, —	33	1,529 1 26	692 10 0	1,069 17 9	757 12 8

IRELAND.

ULSTER. —	1	1 0 33	surrendered,	5 1 0	2 10 0
LEINSTER, —	4	147 8 17	73 0 0	100 16 0	62 10 8
CONNAUGHT, —	5	53 2 19	17 15 0	19 7 6	13 0 0
MUNSTER, —	36	1,389 1 36	692 10 0	1,069 17 9	767 12 6
TOTALS, —	48	1,597 0 15	783 5 0	1,185 2 8	864 12 2

LEASEHOLDERS.

SUMMARY FOR MARCH, 1892.

Summary showing, according to Provinces and Counties, the Number of Cases in which Judicial Rents have been Fixed by Chief Commission and Sub-Commissions under the Land Law (Ireland) Act, 1887, during the Month of March, 1892; and also the Acreages, Tenement Valuations, Former Rents, and Judicial Rents of the Holdings.

Province and County.	Number of Cases in which Judicial Rents have been fixed.	Acreage.			Tenement Valuation.			Former Rent.			Judicial Rent.		
		A.	R.	P.	£	s.	d.	£	s.	d.	£	s.	d.
ULSTER—													
Antrim,	91	430	3	23	343	0	0	341	4	2½	299	1	7
Cavan,	1	12	0	31	8	13	0	14	3	6	10	0	0
Donegal,	8	173	1	7	165	0	0	150	0	0	186	10	0
Tyrone,	6	131	0	0	118	10	0	121	10	0	84	5	0
Total,	29	847	0	31	634	11	0	626	17	7½	335	16	3
LEINSTER—													
Carlow,	1	3	3	34	3	0	0	7	0	0	2	0	0
Dublin,	3	63	3	23	63	0	0	136	13	0	103	0	0
Kildare,	1	749	2	10	811	10	0	698	0	10	498	0	10
Kilkenny,	1	213	3	17	210	10	0	309	14	0	213	16	0
King's,	10	778	0	31	101	13	0	349	13	8	212	13	11
Meath,	17	2,052	0	18	2,193	10	0	2,543	7	11½	2,104	0	0
Westmeath,	1	10	0	23	7	10	0	4	0	0	3	0	0
Wexford,	13	946	3	37	363	5	0	606	5	1	607	15	0
Wicklow,	1	33	0	5	37	0	0	10	0	0	30	0	0
Total,	48	4,551	2	30	3,001	0	0	4,502	11	6½	3,680	1	8
CONNAUGHT—													
Galway,	1	30	0	0	13	0	0	13	0	2	12	0	0
Leitrim,	3	63	3	16	37	13	0	12	10	0	32	15	0
Roscommon,	10	561	3	37	309	10	0	191	13	4	154	13	5
Total,	14	677	3	3	360	5	0	257	3	6	199	7	4
MUNSTER—													
Limerick,	1	29	3	23	31	0	0	43	0	0	79	10	0
Tipperary,	1	34	1	0	39	10	0	37	0	0	45	0	0
Total,	3	63	3	23	70	10	0	80	0	0	74	10	0

IRELAND.

ULSTER,	29	847	0	31	634	11	0	626	17	7½	335	16	3
LEINSTER,	48	4,551	2	30	3,601	0	0	4,502	11	6½	3,680	1	6
CONNAUGHT,	14	677	3	5	360	5	0	257	2	6	199	7	4
MUNSTER,	3	63	3	23	70	10	0	80	0	0	74	10	0
TOTALS,	91	6,160	0	86	4,567	6	0	3,485	11	8	4,489	15	8

CIVIL BILL COURTS.

LEASEHOLDERS.

SUMMARY FOR MARCH, 1892.

Cases in which Judicial Rents have been fixed by Civil Bill Courts, under the Land Law (Ireland) Act, 1887, and notified to the Irish Land Commission during the Month of March, 1892.

Province and County	Number of Cases in which Judicial Rents have been Fixed.	Area	Rent	Former Rent.	Judicial Rent.
		Statute Acres.			
		A. R. P.	£ s. d.	£ s. d.	£ s. d.
CONNAUGHT—					
Leitrim, ...	10	151 3 11	103 12 0	107 17 4	73 14 0
MUNSTER—					
Kerry, ...	3	53 3 33	23 10 0	42 12 0	30 16 0
Limerick, ...	4	259 3 15	131 13 0	197 15 9	140 13 0
Total, ...	7	319 3 8	157 3 0	310 7 2	171 2 0

IRELAND.

CONNAUGHT, ...	10	151 3 11	103 12 0	107 17 4	73 14 0
MUNSTER, ...	7	312 8 8	157 5 0	240 7 2	171 3 0
Total, ...	17	764 2 19	260 17 0	348 4 6	244 16 0

IRISH LAND COMMISSION.

PROVINCE OF

COUNTY OF

Names of Assistant Commissioners by whom Cases were decided	No.	Name of Tenant	Name of Landlord	Townland
Assistant Commissioners— K. GILL (Legal). A. R. MONTGOMERY. M. JOHNSTON.	4408	William McComb,	William Thompson,	Ballyhegaldrick,
	4409	John Mallroy,	James Gray and anor., Trustees of Major George Gray.	Killymurrs,
	4410	Joseph Dunlop,	James R. Moore,	Tullyhlagh,
	4411	Harper Wauson,	Robert T. Crawford and ors,	Moneydoff,
	4412	Rebecca Coleman,	William McKeon,	Curraluey,
	4413	Thomas Aicken,	John Campbell and another,	do.
	4414	William Buchanan,	Mrs. Jane Drummond,	Wildewney,
	4415	Patrick Laverty,	Right Honorable John Young and another, Trustees of Thomas Hamilton,	Ballyturgan,
	4416	William Kennahan,	John Lanyon and another,	Legnagooley,
	4417	John Clinton,	do.	do.
	4418	William Walkon,	Charles McD. Stuart and anor., Trustees of James Hanta,	Magheraboy,
	4419	Elizabeth Ball,	do,	do.
	4420	William Morrow,	John S. Alexander,	Tanloghtmore,
	4421	John McMullan,	Lord O'Neil,	Muckram,
	4422	Patrick O'Neill,	do.	Killmurry,
	4423	James R. Dickson,	do.	Broughshane,
	4424	Do.	do.	do.
				Total,

COUNTY OF

E. GREEN (Legal). J. H. McDANELL. R. W. CRAWOR.	8673	Bridget Curtin,	John Cushman,	Ruakey, Upper,
	8674	Joseph McBeth,	Earl of Erne,	Ballindrum and another,
	8675	William Buchanan,	Charles J. L. Bucknall,	Croghan,
	8676	Margaret Eaton, Ltd. Admnst. of Ephraim Eaton,	Alexander M. Servant,	Montanyeny,
	8677	John Connelly,	do.	do.

ULSTER.

ANTRIM.

Extent of Holding. Statute.	Poor Law Valuation.	Former Rent.	Judicial Rent.	Observations.	Term of Tenancy.
A. R. P.	£ s. d.	£ s. d.	£ s. d.		£ s. d.
81 1 8	14 10 0	25 0 0	20 0 0		
5 3 10	1 0 0	3 0 0	1 10 0		
81 0 3	9 10 0	13 15 0	11 0 0		
25 0 0	18 0 0	14 0 0	18 10 0		
18 8 0	17 10 0	23 8 10	14 5 0		
5 3 33	10 0 0	10 15 0	9 10 0		
1 2 33	9 10 0	10 5 10	7 10 0		
50 0 0	35 0 0	38 9 5½	30 0 0		
17 1 13	16 5 0	16 10 0	8 0 0		
16 3 11	8 10 0	15 10 0	5 0 0		
15 0 0	10 0 0	10 4 0	8 0 0		
25 0 0	20 15 0	17 5 0	17 5 0		
32 0 0	31 15 0	22 5 0	36 13 0		
74 3 28	13 15 0	9 15 2	9 0 0		
23 0 0	33 0 0	31 17 0	31 17 0		
2 0 16	unascertained.	8 17 5	8 0 0		

Names of Assistant Commissioners by whom Cases were decided.	No.	Name of Tenant.	Name of Landlord.
Assistant Commissioners—			
W. F. Bailey (Legal).	8678	Michael Mulhern, ...	Patrick Rafferty, ...
T. A. Dillon.	8679	Do., ...	do.
T. Davidson.	8680	John Johnston, ...	do.
	8681	Patrick McMann, ...	do.

DONEGAL—continued.

Extent of Holding. Statute.	Poor Law Valuation.	Former Rent.	Judicial Rent.	Observations.	Value of Tenancy.
A. R. P.	£ s. d.	£ s. d.	£ s. d.		£ s. d.
6 1 6	6 10 0	7 10 0	5 0 0		
16 1 35	16 0 0	13 0 0	11 0 0		
19 1 20	15 10 0	18 8 0	14 13 0		
18 1 34	13 0 0	10 4 4	9 0 0		
176 1 87	128 10 0	125 15 10	84 9 0		

FERMANAGH.

18 8 10	6 6 0	9 13 10	7 5 0	By agreem.	
23 3 16	7 10 0	7 0 0	6 0 0	do.	
20 2 25	7 0 0	6 18 0	5 13 6	do.	
68 3 11	72 16 0	22 3 10	16 16 6		

TYRONE.

COUNTY OF

Names of Assistant Commissioners by whom Cases were decided.	No.	Name of Tenant.	Name of Landlord.	Townland.
Assistant Commissioners— R. GRACE, (Legal). J. H. McCONNELL. R. W. CRAWFORD.	1854	John Jameson,	F. A. Moore and another,	Revells,
	1853	John Logan,	George Hall Stack,	Aldishoburn,
	1856	James McShane,	do.	do.
	1857	Hugh Conway,	do.	do.
				Tuml,

PROVINCE OF

COUNTY OF

	No.			
Assistant Commissioners— R. R. NASH (Legal). J. HARBISON. A. M. CRETH.	951	William Colony,	Madam Morris,	Killealackey,

COUNTY OF

TYRONE—*continued.*

Extent of Holding Statute.	Poor Law Valuation.	Former Rent.	Judicial Rent.	
a. r. p.	£ s. d.	£ s. d.	£ s. d.	
8 1 0	3 15 0	12 0 0	8 0 0	
13 7 30	4 10 0	5 10 0	5 15 0	
16 3 0	7 0 0	7 0 0	6 10 0	
7 0 26	unascertained	3 1 0	1 8 0	
765 0 83	975 14 0	613 11 0	544 14 0	

LEINSTER.

KILDARE.

9 1 35	6 15 0	7 15 0	5 15 0	

KILKENNY.

19 0 5	15 10 0	14 5 0	14 4 0	The rate occupied of the

COUNTY.

Names of Assistant Commissioners by whom Cases were decided.	No.	Name of Tenant	Name of Landlord	Townland.
Assistant Commissioners—				
B. B. Lane (Legal)	1711	William Donnelly, ...	Richard Warburton, ...	Rathmore, ...
J. Haughton.	1712	John Larkin, —	do. ..	do. ...
A. B. Crotty.	1713	Thomas Maloney & otrs.	do. ...	Annagra, ...
	1714	Thomas McNamara, ...	do. ...	do. ...
	1715	William Dunne, ...	do. ...	Rathmore, ...
	1716	Peter Dempsey, ...	do. ..	Annagra, ...
	1717	Thomas Wyse & anor.,	do. ..	Grahtycannon, ...
	1718	James Strong, junior, continued in names of Wm. Dowrell and another.	do. —	Rierratoghie, ...
	1719	John Gannell, —	Eyre Evans Edwards and Jessie Edwards, lunatic, by Ernest de J. Brown their committee.	Tinena, —
	1720	Patrick Geoghegan, —	Mrs. Catherine Geoghegan, —	Feerboy, ...
	1721	Charles Malloy, junior,	M. J. Brisson, ...	Rathmoreand snpr.
	1722	Timothy Cornwell, ...	J. J. Hubert Fox, —	Aughabahry, —
	1723	Michael Glennon, —	William Glennon, ...	Ballyfarrell —
	1724	James Carey, ...	William O'Connor Morris, ...	Gortnamona, —
	1725	Francis Stanley, —	Lord Digby, —	Gortnera, ...
	1726	Anne Hand, ...	Henry Chenevix, ...	Brochia, Little,
	1727	Stephen Conroy, ...	Rev. Thomas Wakerell, ...	Castletown, —
	1728	Mary Minnock, ...	T. C. Franks and P. G. Smyley,	Ballom, ...
	1729	William Cronin, ...	Rev. Richard Clarke, ...	Tinnarnough, ...
				Total, ...

COUNTY—*continued.*

Names of Holding, Barony	Poor Law Valuation.	Former Rent.	Judicial Rent.	Observations.	Value of Tenancy.
A. R. P.	£ s. d.	£ s. d.	£ s. d.		£ s. d.
14 0 31	5 3 0	7 14 6	5 0 0		
9 3 71	8 5 0	9 4 0	6 5 0		
53 0 11	30 15 0	54 0 0	30 0 0		
3 3 26	1 16 0	3 8 5	2 0 0		
16 3 9	6 15 0	9 8 10	7 0 0		
14 0 23	8 5 0	7 16 11	6 0 0		
106 3 15	45 0 0	70 0 0	13 0 0		
12 5 37	13 10 0	10 5 6	11 13 0	And right of grazing 7 sellups on Barraburgh Bog.	
11 3 14	6 0 0	9 5 4	5 10 0		
6 0 11	3 5 0	6 0 0	5 0 0		
50 3 29	27 14 0	33 15 0	30 0 0		
5 1 73	2 15 0	3 11 0	3 11 0		
9 2 9	—	3 0 0	3 0 0		
20 3 0	11 5 6	14 10 0	11 5 0		
106 3 18	42 0 0	50 5 0	43 0 0		
50 0 0	8 13 0	9 8 0	7 15 0		
17 2 0	7 0 0	10 0 0	7 17 6		
5 3 24	1 10 0	3 8 9	1 17 4		
9 0 21	6 5 0	8 10 0	6 5 0	By contract	
700 2 2	197 17 0	439 8 7	852 2 10		

MEATH.

79 3 21	171 0 0	140 0 0	177 0 0	By contract.	
34 3 18	61 0 0	44 4 4	44 4 4		
854 3 33	343 10 0	350 0 0	350 0 0		
13 0 10	6 15 0	8 16 4	6 0 0		
4 3 12	8 5 0	6 16 10	5 6 0		
84 3 26	55 5 0	44 0 0	33 0 0		
6 1 15	10 5 0	19 13 8	9 0 0		
411 2 10	456 0 0	508 17 4	654 11 6		

Names of Assistant Commissioners by whom Cases were decided.	No.	Name of Tenant.	Name of Landlord.	Townland.
Assistant Commissioners— R. R. Kane (Legal). M. F. Lynch. L. Ormsby.	2296	Peter Kennedy,	Rev. William Donolan and another.	Stonhard,
	3796	Richard Slamon,	Earl of Portsmouth,	Clones,
	1897	Arthur Bochn,	do.	Killereogan,
	1338	Patrick Furlonn,	do.	do.
R. R. Kane (Legal). L. Ormsby.	2799	John Bishop,	William Phaire,	Templeanby,
	2800	Michael Doyle,	Robert W. Hall Dare,	Ballintquark,
				Total,

Assistant Commissioners—	No.	Name of Tenant.	Name of Landlord.	Townland.
R. R. Kane (Legal). C. R. Butler. P. Callan.	8898	Catherine Coughlan,	W. A. R. Usher and another,	Dundongan,
	8894	Anne Grogan, Limtd. Admix. of John Grogan.	do.	Rasteril Peak,
	8897	John Quinn,	John Charvers,	Lissill West,
	8898	Ellen Geraghty, Limtd. Admix. of Michael Geraghty,	Captain John H. Blakeney,	Lehanagh,
	8899	James Skarra,	do.	Gallagh,
	8900	Martin Higgins,	Peter J. Crolan and another,	do.
	8901	Pat Connolly,	do.	do.
	8902	John Haverty, Limtd. Admr. of Michael Haverty.	do.	do.
	8903	Honor Doonlan,	do.	do.
	8904	Michael Curtis,	do.	do.
	8905	Mary Dolan,	John O'Connor,	Ballyclogan,
	8906	James Loughnane,	H. J. C. Martin and another,	Carrahurn,
	8907	Andrew Killilea,	do.	Cloonabrisks,
	8908	John Shaughnessy and another	do.	Ballinacreagh,
	8909	John Shaughnessy,	do.	Lissalouagh,
	8910	Conner Reab, junior,	Henry J. Ekin,	Annaghmore West

WEXFORD.

Area of holding	Poor Law Valuation	Former Rent	Judicial Rent	Observations	Value of Tenancy
A. R. P.	£ s. d.	£ s. d.	£ s. d.		£ s. d.
50 2 37	29 10 0	20 5 8	20 0 0	By consent	
71 3 13	30 10 0	34 0 0	30 0 0	do.	
55 0 5	ascertained	29 10 0	23 15 0	do.	
35 0 17	do.	11 0 0	10 10 0	do.	
33 0 37	11 0 0	20 0 0	18 0 0	do.	
3 0 10	3 0 0	4 17 0	3 0 0	do.	
717 3 37	76 0 0	133 12 8	108 9 0		

CONNAUGHT.

GALWAY.

3 1 6	3 10 0	3 16 11	8 0 0		
6 1 0	7 10 0	6 0 6	3 7 6		
7 1 24	4 15 0	6 7 6	6 0 0		
6 2 26	2 0 0	3 5 0	3 5 0		
9 3 20	1 15 0	2 4 4	3 0 0		
7 2 23	unascertained	4 0 0	3 0 0		
6 3 6	do.	1 15 0	3 15 0		
10 1 22	3 15 0	1 0 0	3 10 0		
15 5 19	unascertained	3 0 0	4 10 0		
13 3 10	do.	6 15 0	8 0 0		
1 1 0	1 6 0	3 0 0	1 5 0		
0 3 13	5 0 0	4 10 0	1 10 0		
13 3 22	6 2 0	3 5 0	5 5 0		
20 2 0	11 13 0	10 17 6	10 17 6		
22 0 5	16 10 0	11 16 0	11 16 0		
2 3 4	5 6 0	2 15 6	3 10 0	And an undivided ¼ of 22a. 1r. 16r.	

COUNTY OF

Names of Assistant Commissioners by whom Cases were decided.	No.	Name of Tenant.	Name of Landlord.	Townland.
Assistant Commissioners—				
R. D. KANE (Legal). C. B. BUTLER. F. CALLAN.	5911	John Gordon, ...	Henry J. Blake, ...	Annaghmore, West
	5912	Garrett Rush, junior, ...	do. ...	do.
	5913	Thomas Walsh, ...	do. ...	do.
	5914	Garrett Rush, ...	do. ...	do.
	5915	James Quinn, ...	Lord Clanbrook, ...	Derrymore,
	5916	Lawrence Murray, ...	do. ...	do.
	5917	Patrick Oakley, ...	do. ...	do.
	5918	Malachy Lally, ...	do. ...	Ballyheen,
	5919	John Reynolds, ...	do. ...	N'Drummore,
	5920	John Carroll, ...	do. ...	do.
	5921	John Skehan, ...	do. ...	Clonagary,
	5922	Lawrence Coigne, ...	do. ...	Raharney,
F. CALLAN. C. R. BUTLER.	5923	Mary Mahern, ...	Stephen Douglas, ...	Lisappol,
	5924	Bridget Finn, ...	Earl of Clonmorty, ...	Ballynavard,
	5925	Richard Sheppard, ...	do. ...	Clonlaughan,
	5926	Patrick Henly, ...	do. ...	Craigavenant,
	5927	Martin Kilken, ...	do. ...	Kilnahern,
	5928	Edward Hall, ...	do. ...	Kellygrove,
	5929	Richard Oakes, ...	do. ...	Urrackree,
				Total,

COUNTY OF

Assistant Commissioners—				
W. F. BAGOT (Legal). T. DAVIDSON. T. A. DILLON.	4570	Martin Wynne, ...	Charles B. Barton, ...	Mullinduff,
	4571	Alexander McVinny, ...	do. ...	Derrinlough,
	4572	Bartley Glancy, ...	Rev. Joseph W. Dickson, Trustee of John B. Dickson.	Gorgrim,
	4573	Thomas Connolly, ...	do. ...	Davley.
	4574	Thomas Burke, ...	Dr. George Ellis, ...	Wardhouse,
	4575	Thomas Gormin, ...	do. ...	do.
	4576	Patrick McGowan, ...	St. George R. Johnston, ...	Aghadarroad,

GALWAY—continued

Extent of Holding. Stat.	Poor Law Valuation.	Former Rent.	Judicial Rent.	Observations.	Value of Tenancy.
A. R. P.	£ s. d.	£ s. d.	£ s. d.		
4 1 37	3 5 0	4 0 0	3 15 0		
9 1 4	1 12 6	2 0 0	2 0 0	And an undivided ⅟₇ of 23a. 1r. 10p.	
5 3 5	4 5 0	5 4 2	4 10 0	And an undivided ¼ of 24a. 1r. 10r.	
2 2 34	4 10 0	4 0 0	3 15 0	And an undivided ¼ of 23a. 1r. 10r.	
12 2 24	5 0 0	4 4 0	4 4 0	Right of grazing 2½ collops on the undivided portion of Derrymore bog.	
17 0 0	5 15 0	8 12 4	9 12 4	Right of grazing 5 collops on the undivided portion of Derrymore bog.	
33 2 4	10 10 0	11 8 5	11 5 0	Right of grazing 5½ collops on the undivided portion of Derrymore bog.	
12 1 5	5 15 0	8 10 0	7 0 0	Right of grazing as heretofore.	
—	uncommitted.	8 15 4	8 15 4	An undivided ¼ of 154a.	
—	uncommitted.	15 5 5	15 6 5	An undivided ¼ of 154a.	
80 0 15	50 15 0	54 0 0	50 0 0		
53 1 21	34 0 0	35 7 0	35 0 0		
51 1 5	26 0 0	47 15 5	25 15 0		
15 3 20	10 10 0	13 5 2	8 7 6		
35 1 10	16 17 0	21 6 5	15 15 0		
43 0 0	11 5 0	26 10 0	16 0 0		
25 0 2	14 10 0	18 5 0	13 5 0		
18 1 18	9 15 0	10 5 5	8 15 0		
46 2 25	23 0 0	27 2 8	23 15 0		
504 2 11	279 16 5	409 18 1	335 11 4		

LEITRIM

Name of Assistant Commissioners by whom Cases were decided.	No.	Name of Tenant.	Name of Landlord.
Assistant Commissioners—			
W. F. Bailey (Legal).	4377	Pat McHugh, ...	Lord Massy, ...
T. Davidson.	4378	Hugh Hann, —	do. —
T. A. Dillon.	4379	Bridget McGarry, —	do. —
	4380	Bridget Finly, —	do. —
	4381	Terence McGovern, —	do. —
	4382	John Gallagher, —	do. —
	4383	James Gallagher, —	do. —
	4384	Peter McGonigle, —	do. —
	4385	Patrick McGovern, —	do. —
	4386	Laurence Park, —	do. —
	4387	James Keany, —	do. —
	4388	John Kerrigan, —	do. —
	4389	Ellen Kerrigan, —	do. —

LEITRIM.—continued.

Extent of Holding, Statute.	Poor Law Valuation.	Former Rent.	Judicial Rent	Observations.	Value of Tenancy.
A. R. P.	£ s. d.	£ s. d.	£ s. d.		£ s. d.
17 7 4	4 10 0	5 0 0	4 12 0		
23 5 34	16 0 0	16 5 0	8 10 0		
13 2 8	7 0 0	7 5 0	6 0 0		
30 3 0	11 4 0	11 4 0	9 0 0		
20 1 7	6 0 0	8 10 10	6 16 0		
64 3 10	7 0 0	9 0 0	6 0 0		
10 0 18	2 5 0	8 0 0	3 0 0		
83 0 31	12 0 0	13 10 0	11 0 0		
7 3 32	5 15 0	6 4 2	5 0 0		
21 0 0	7 17 0	8 0 0	8 10 0		
19 2 1	7 16 0	6 5 0	6 18 0		
23 1 18	4 15 0	7 10 0	4 16 0		
17 3 12	4 15 0	6 0 0	4 10 0		
673 3 1	160 7 0	162 4 0	118 6 0		

ROSCOMMON.

10 3 34	8 5 0	9 10 0	7 7 0		
8 0 8	3 0 0	2 8 0	1 16 0		
6 0 23	6 0 0	6 10 0	6 8 5		
8 0 7	8 5 0	7 12 0	6 16 0		
21 1 30	10 15 0	13 0 0	8 5 0		
10 3 0	2 15 0	1 10 0	1 10 0	By agent A	
3 0 0	0 10 0	0 10 0	0 16 0	do.	
73 0 0	10 5 0	8 5 5	9 5 5	do.	
61 3 10	20 0 0	9 8 5	9 5 8	do.	
13 1 17	3 0 0	3 16 0	2 16 0	do.	
63 0 18	14 15 0	13 0 0	17 0 0	do.	
26 1 17	8 0 0	4 10 0	6 10 0	do.	
15 1 6	1 15 0	1 10 0	1 10 0	do.	
11 3 0	2 8 0	3 3 0	3 0 0	do.	
10 3 33	5 0 0	9 15 0	9 16 0	do.	
11 0 33	4 8 0	5 17 0	5 17 0	do.	
6 1 10	1 10 0	1 5 0	1 0 2	do.	

Name of Assistant Commissioner by whom Claim was decided.	No.	Name of Tenant.	Name of Landlord.	Townland.
Assistant Commissioners—				
W. F. Bailey (Legal), T. McAlfen, L. W. Byrne	6687	James Dunne,	H. R. O'Connor,	Leragh,
	6688	Dominick Larkin,	do.	do.
	6689	Michael Conlon,	do.	Garrentemple More,
	6690	William Connolly,	do.	do.
	6691	Catherine Connolly,	do.	do.
	6692	Martin Leech,	do.	do.
	6693	James Connor,	do.	do.
	6694	Honoria Giblin,	H. R. P. Malone,	Tully,
	6695	Michael Donnellan,	do.	Ballintolughan,
	6696	Anthony Veasy,	do.	do.
	6697	Michael Veasy,	do.	do. (Owen),
	6698	Patrick Ward,	do.	Ra.Nualstinghan,
	6699	Hugh Reddy,	do.	do.
	6700	Bridget Veasy, Ltd. Admr. of Andrew Veasy.	do.	do.
	6701	Patrick Tighe,	do.	do.
	6702	Thomas Crean,	do.	Carlis,
	6703	Thomas McDermott,	do.	do.
	6704	Patrick Lynch,	do.	do.
	6705	Bridget Flinn,	do.	do.
	6706	James Kelly,	do.	do.
	6707	Connor Commons,	do.	Castlecois,
	6708	Joseph Kenny,	do.	Castlenagole,
	6709	John White,	do.	Rusllck and same.
	6710	Patrick Kelly,	do.	Carlis,
	6711	Patrick Veasy,	do.	do.
	6712	Patrick Reilly,	do.	Currowbane,
	6713	Helen Henton,	Mrs. Harriett Dickson, sued in the name of Mrs. Harriett Barron.	Cahir,
	6714	Pat Walsh,	do.	Pourghill,
	6715	Patrick Brennan,	do.	do.
	6716	James Flanagan,	do.	do.
	6717	Cath. Kelly, Limited Ad.	do.	do.

ROSCOMMON—*continued*

Extent of Holding. Statute.	Poor Law Valuation.	Former Rent.	Judicial Rent.	Observations.	Years of Tenancy.
a. r. p.	£ s. d.	£ s. d.	£ s. d.		£ s. d.
7 3 15	8 10 0	7 0 0	6 5 0		
19 3 25	17 0 0	16 14 0	13 0 0		
6 1 35	8 15 0	4 10 6	8 0 0		
3 2 8	unascertained.	1 15 3	1 1 0		
3 3 11	do.	1 18 0	0 18 0		
6 1 1	do.	1 17 6	1 2 6		
8 3 57	1 5 0	2 17 0	1 2 6		
54 0 10	25 15 0	28 8 6	34 0 0		
72 0 5	43 0 0	40 0 0	22 0 0		
24 3 14	8 13 0	5 10 0	5 10 0		
16 2 00	8 0 0	6 10 5	4 7 6		
16 1 30	unascertained.	5 2 5	4 0 0		
16 2 20	8 0 0	6 7 0	3 19 6		
10 2 15	5 10 0	6 2 6	3 10 0		
21 0 22	10 5 0	11 7 0	6 5 0		
10 2 26	12 15 0	16 1 4	13 0 0		
22 2 0	10 10 0	15 1 5	11 0 0		
22 2 0	unascertained.	10 0 0	6 16 0		
11 1 0	0 10 0	6 7 6	7 18 0		
55 2 10	unascertained.	33 8 0	29 0 0		
17 0 10	5 0 0	6 2 4	5 5 0		
21 0 10	10 10 0	11 11 4	7 15 0		
14 0 0	7 5 0	10 11 0	7 6 0		
22 2 20	unascertained.	6 0 0	7 6 0		
11 0 6	0 5 0	5 5 0	6 12 8		
16 1 10	8 10 0	14 4 0	6 0 0		
22 2 0	9 10 0	11 15 0	7 16 0		
15 1 0	4 15 0	6 0 0	6 7 6	With right of grazing with three others over 56a. 2r.	
82 3 5	6 10 0	7 15 6	4 11 5		
16 0 20	7 0 0	7 16 0	5 5 0		
10 2 20	3 16 0	6 0 0	3 5 0		
26 0 20	8 5 0	7 10 0	6 5 0		
12 2 15	5 0 0	6 10 0	6 0 0	do.	
25 2 1	7 0 0	7 5 0	6 0 0		

COUNTY OF

Name of Assistant Commissioners by whom Cases were decided.	No.	Name of Tenant.	Name of Landlord.		Townland.	
Assistant Commissioners— W. F. Bailey (Legal). T. McAfee. L. W. Byrne.	6731	James Connolly, ...	Mrs. Harriett Dickson, coutd. in name of Mrs. Harriett Eastwd.		Fonghill,	—
	6732	Pat Connolly,	...	do.	—	...	do.	—
	6733	Michael McGovern,	—	do.	...	...	do.	—
	6734	Patrick Gunning,	...	do.	...	...	do.	—
	6735	Luke Kelly, —	...	do.	—	...	do.	—
	6736	John Kelly, ...	...	do.	—	...	do.	—
	6737	Martin Flynn,	...	do.	...	—	do.	—
	6738	John Bligh, ...	—	do.	...	...	Clonmron,	—
	6739	Widow Cath. Coughlin,		do.	...	—	Clonough,	—
	5730	John Manden,	...	do.	...	...	do.	—
	6731	Martin Henier,	...	do.	...	—	do.	—
	6732	Pat Harte, —	—	do.	...	—	do.	—.
	6733	Anne Coughlin,	—	do.	...	...	do.	—
						Total,	—

CIVIL BILL

PROVINCE OF
COUNTY OF

County Court Judge.	No.	Name of Tenant.	Name of Landlord.		Townland.	
J. C. Neligan, &c.	301	Andrew Machle,	...	Lucinda McKinerey,	—	Ballygurk,	...

PROVINCE OF
COUNTY OF

ROSCOMMON—*continued.*

Extent of Holding in Statute	Poor Law Valuation.	Former Rent.	Judicial Rent.	Observations.	Value of Tenant's
A. R. P.	£ s. d.	£ s. d.	£ s. d.		£ s. d.
28 1 15	11 5 0	16 0 0	6 5 0		
30 0 12	13 0 0	16 18 2	9 12 0		
5 2 30	2 0 0	3 0 0	1 17 0		
29 1 13	6 10 0	9 0 0	6 10 0		
19 0 16	5 0 0	7 10 0	1 11 0		
9 2 20	3 0 0	5 18 0	2 12 0		
14 1 10	4 10 0	6 16 0	3 7 6		
41 1 0	13 10 0	18 0 0	11 6 0		
17 0 25	8 10 0	9 17 6	7 5 0		
4 1 0	3 0 0	5 15 0	1 15 0		
13 0 13	6 10 0	7 10 0	6 15 0		
7 2 31	4 5 0	6 0 0	3 17 6		
17 3 6	6 15 0	9 12 6	7 6 0		
1,316 2 35	434 10 0	653 15 6	409 15 3		

COURTS.

ULSTER.

LONDONDERRY.

Extent of Holding in Statute	Poor Law Valuation.	Former Rent.	Judicial Rent.	Observations	Value of Tenant's.
A. R. P.	£ s. d.	£ s. d.	£ s. d.		£ s. d.
1 0 33	unappropriated,	5 1 0	2 10 0		

LEINSTER·

CARLOW.

COUNTY OF

County Court Judge.	No.	Name of Tenant.	Name of Landlord.	Townland.
W. F. Darley, q.c.	4	Richard Daly, ...	Col. D. Hunt and another, ...	The Ridge, ...
	5	Peter Kavanagh, ...	do.	Knockinan, ...
				Total, ...

PROVINCE OF

COUNTY OF

Gilbert Wrren, q.c.	1115	John Scanlon, ..	Mary T. Meehan and another,	Drumminna, ..
	1116	Thomas Nolan, ...	Wm. Brady and others, Trusts. of John Brady.	Knockagan, —
	1117	Mary Wynne, ...	Sarah A. Tottenham, ...	Killydagher, —
	1118	James Kenny, ..	do.	do. —
	1119	Hugh Callan, ...	do.	do. —
				Total, —

PROVINCE OF

CARLOW—*continued.*

Extent of Holding in Statute Acres.	Poor Law Valuation.	Former Rent.	Judicial Rent.	Observations.
A. R. P.	£ s. d.	£ s. d.	£ s. d.	
37 2 34	15 10 0	21 5 0	16 0 0	By agreement.
8 0 15	0 15 0	2 10 0	2 0 0	do.
161 3 27	73 0 0	100 16 0	82 10 6	

CONNAUGHT.

LEITRIM.

7 0 0	4 10 0	6 1 9	5 5 0	By agreement.
6 1 0	4 5 0	4 15 6	5 5 0	
13 2 24	2 0 6	2 0 0	1 10 0	
13 0 0	3 5 0	3 10 4	3 5 0	
15 2 35	5 15 0	4 10 0	4 5 0	
56 3 10	17 15 0	19 7 6	18 0 0	

MUNSTER.

COUNTY OF

County Court Judge.	No.	Name of Tenant.	Name of Landlord.	Townland.
J. J. Shaw, q.c.	478	Cornelius Crowley, —	Henry A. Herbert, ...	Knockilelly, —
	479	John Fuller, —	James R. J. Julien, ...	Lamperaghan, ...
	480	Patrick Quilter, a lunatic, by Mary Talbot & anor.	Sir Francis Blackwood, ...	Gneeshavoreen,
	481	Edmond O'Connor, ...	George R. Mevrue, ...	Shrone, Kent, and another.
	482	Timothy Linihan and another.	Francis M. Norcott and anor.,	Parknasilloge,
	483	Michael Duggan & anor.,	Elizabeth Fitzgerald, ...	Meenkrens, ...
	484	David W. Curtin, ...	James H. Dunn, ...	Aleen, —
	485	John Lucas, ...	Lord Headley and another, ...	Meenlaterane, ...
	486	Francis Twiss and anor.,	Francis M. Norcott and anor.,	Parknasilloge,
	487	Patrick Shea, —	John Bateman, ...	Gharagum, —
	488	William O'Connor, —	Ross T. Houghton, ...	Kavelamorra, —
	489	John B. O'Connor, ...	do. —	do.
	490	Mary Carroty, —	do. ...	Ilsamore, —
	491	Edmond Sappio, —	do. —	Knockmaree and another.
	492	Theodore Foley, —	William L. Roe, —	Reragen, ...
	493	Michael Cahill, —	do. —	do. —
	494	John Sugrue, —	Sir Robert A. Denny, ...	Ballygarran, —
	495	Patrick Dillane, —	do. —	Kantedmahalon, —
	496	James Donaghan, —	do. ...	Dough, ...
				Total. —

COUNTY OF

KERRY.

Amount of Holding Statute	Poor Law Valuation	Former Rent	Judicial Rent	Observations	Value of Tenancy
A. R. P.	£ s. d.	£ s. d.	£ s. d.		£ s. d.
125 9 14	9 0 0	18 0 0	15 0 0		
17 3 20	14 5 0	22 17 1	16 18 0		
106 3 11	28 15 0	40 0 0	34 10 0		
100 1 28	43 0 0	46 0 0	77 10 0		
10 2 17	5 0 0	0 10 0	8 0 0		
13 3 0	unsurveyed land	1 0 0	8 0 0		
34 0 3	10 10 0	18 0 0	9 0 0		
43 2 10	9 5 0	12 17 6	10 5 0		
45 0 0	16 10 0	21 13 0	14 0 0		
38 0 0	5 15 0	8 10 0	7 0 0		
4 0 26	1 0 0	4 15 0	8 10 0		
9 3 16	1 15 0	4 10 0	2 7 8		
16 3 29	5 0 0	13 0 0	7 0 0		
14 1 24	4 15 0	7 0 0	5 0 0		
9 2 31	0 15 0	2 8 8	9 0 0		
9 3 25	1 15 0	3 0 0	3 5 0		
73 1 24	43 5 0	45 0 0	49 0 0		
34 0 35	11 10 0	17 0 0	15 0 0		
45 2 5	12 15 0	18 0 0	15 0 0		
765 2 39	230 10 0	344 18 1	379 17 8		

LIMERICK.

LAND LAW (IRELAND) ACT, 1887.

LEASEHOLDERS.

Names of Assistant Commissioners by whom Cases were decided	No.	Name of Tenant.	Name of Landlord.	Townland.
HEAD COMMISSION.	1544	David McElveen, ...	Earl of Antrim, — ...	Glenwillan, ...
	1545	William Lewis, sued in name of Robert Joseph Lewis, assignee of Wm. Lewis.	Sir R. Wallace, Bart., sued, after death of the said Sir R. Wallace, Bart., in the name of Dame Amelia Julia Charlotte Wallace, his successor in title.	Part of Berrigan,
R. GREER (Legal). A. R. MONTGOMERY. H. JELLETT.	1546	Patrick Nesson, ...	Lord O'Neill, — ...	Lower Broughshane.
	1547	James Crawford, ...	Edward McS. H. Pelham, ...	Ballyshieughan, —
	1548	Robert L. Paul, —	James Gray and anor., Trustees of Major George Gray.	N Clynverran, —
	1549	Joseph Gregg, junior, ...	James S. Mason, — ...	Fromen, —
	1550	Gavin Gregg, ...	do.	do. —
	1551	Hugh Kyle, ...	do.	do. —
	1552	John Lake, —	do. — ...	do. —
	1553	Do. — —	do. — —	do. —
	1554	Joseph Gregg, —	do. — ...	do. —
	1555	James Ross, —	do. — ...	do. —
	1556	Robert Stewart, —	do. — ...	do. —
	1557	Samuel Linton & another,	do. — —	do. —
	1558	William J. Robinson, —	John Smith and anor., Trustees of Robert Crawford.	Ruland,
	1559	John Gray, —	do.	do. —
	1560	James Owens and anor.,	do. — —	Lismahill,
	1561	Robert Johnston, ...	do. — —	do. —
	1562	Do. ... —	do. — —	do. —
	1563	James Thompson, ...	do. — —	Ruland,
	1564	Edward Harvey, —	Earl of Antrim, — ...	Kilmore,
				Tual, —

ULSTER.

ANTRIM.

Extent of Holdings.	Poor Law Valuation.	Former Rent.	Judicial Rent.	Observations.
a. r. p.	£ s. d.	£ s. d.	£ s. d.	
139 0 36	91 6 0	64 7 10	57 0 0	And an equivalent portion of certain containing 163 acres or more. The rent in this case was fixed by consent of the parties, the sitting of the Court in Dublin.
9 0 53	10 0 0	7 0 0	3 8 0	The rent in this case was fixed consent of the parties at the sitting of the Court in Dublin.
31 0 80	43 15 0	27 5 2	27 4 2	
18 3 17	14 0 0	14 5 0	13 0 0	And 1½ acres on mountain.
0 0 0	unascertained.	7 11 10	6 8 0	
12 0 17	10 0 0	8 15 0	7 12 0	And pasturage over 6a. 1r. 5½
19 1 0	13 10 0	12 3 0	11 0 0	
21 1 6	unascertained.	14 12 6	13 10 0	
13 0 19	8 10 0	8 4 0	8 10 0	And right of pasturage over 6 ac of bog.
18 1 3	9 10 0	8 13 5	8 0 0	do.
63 3 37	17 0 0	21 0 0	17 5 0	And right of pasturage over 11 ac of bog.
17 0 14	9 15 0	9 9 4	8 0 0	
23 0 18	14 5 0	12 17 0	11 15 0	
19 2 27	unascertained.	15 10 0	15 0 0	
16 0 39	10 5 0	11 0 0	9 15 0	
23 3 0	13 5 0	15 0 0	10 0 0	
62 0 25	23 0 0	23 0 0	20 10 0	
18 3 33	11 0 0	11 0 0	8 16 0	
31 3 0	12 0 0	12 0 0	10 5 0	
4 1 16	3 5 0	4 10 0	3 5 0	
41 1 16	37 0 0	33 13 10½	30 0 0	By consent.
810 2 89	345 6 0	341 4 2½	279 1 2	

CAVAN.

Name of Assistant Commissioners by whom Case was Settled.	No.	Name of Tenant.	Name of Landlord.	Townland.
Assistant Commissioners—				
R. Gibson (Legal). J. M. McDevitt. R. W. Crabbe.	439	Joseph MacBeth, ...	Earl of Erne, ...	Menina, ...
	421	Elizabeth McConaghey,	Rev. John R. Verschoyle and another.	Tullydangel, ...
				Total, ...

Assistant Commissioners—				
R. Gibson (Legal). J. M. McDevitt. R. W. Crabbe.	781	Matthew Kerr and anor.,	Paul Holmes, ...	Magtrr, ...
	782	Richard Fair, ...	General A. Moore,	Garvin Elgrum,
	783	Samuel McGrra, ...	Duke of Abercorn, ...	Loughanan, ...
	784	Do., ...	do.	Ballylaw, ...
	785	John Cunningham,	do.	Gortanven, ...
				Total, ...

PROVINCE OF

Assistant Commissioners—				
R. R. Kane (Legal). L. Corbit.	447	Henry Porter, ...	Caroline Finlay, ...	Cross, ...

DONEGAL.

Extent of Holding, Statute.	Poor Law Valuation.	Former Rent.	Judicial Rent.	Observations.	Value of Tenancy.
A. R. P.	£ s. d.	£ s. d.	£ s. d.		£ s. d.
102 3 28	100 0 0	80 0 0	72 0 0		
70 1 19	65 0 0	70 0 0	58 10 0		
173 1 7	165 0 0	150 0 0	130 10 0		

TYRONE.

9 0 33	14 10 0	80 0 0	19 15 0		
13 3 8	11 0 0	10 17 6	8 15 0		
56 0 0	31 5 0	27 8 1	13 15 0		
38 1 20	26 0 0	23 10 4	23 10 0		
13 3 10	33 15 0	59 14 1	25 10 0		
131 0 0	116 10 0	131 10 0	96 5 0		

LEINSTER.

CARLOW.

3 3 25	2 0 0	8 0 0	8 0 0		

DUBLIN.

COUNTY OF

Name of Assistant Commissioners by whom Cases were decided.	No.	Name of Tenant.	Name of Landlord.	Townland.
Head Commission.	505	Edward Robinson,	General George W. T. Rich,	Kilmily & anr.

COUNTY OF

Head Commission.	579	Thomas Kidd,	W. H. Ford,	Darmaburgh and another.

KING'S

R. R. Kane (Legal). J. Haughton. A. N. Orpen.	531	Martin McEvoy,	Frank Sandars,	Draytown,
	532	Patrick Gorden,	Charles Blackney,	Silverbrook,
	533	George Black,	Henry P. Rhodes,	Kilmoony,
	534	Patrick Conlan,	Frederick W. Russell,	Palmon,
	535	John Holton,	David Sherlock,	Newtown,
	536	Michael Kenny and Catherine Kenny,	do.	Derrynaller,
	537	Michael Kenny and Catherine Kenny,	J. J. H. Fox,	Aughinlacky,
	538	Terence Grennan, Ltd. Admen. of Patrick Grennan, deceased,	William O'Connor Morris,	Mucaghdarmot,
	539	John Mahon, Ltd. Admer. of Patrick Mahon, decd.	do.	Ballinamny,
	540	Michael Bermingham,	Col. D. Smith, and Mrs. D. F. Andrews,	Kilpatrick,
				Total,

COUNTY OF

TABLE OF JUDICIAL RENTS

KILDARE.

Extent of Holding Statute.	Poor Law Valuation.	Former Rent.	Judicial Rent.	Observations.
A. R. P.	£ s. d.	£ s. d.	£ s. d.	
749 2 10	611 10 0	520 0 10	475 0 10	The rent, &c., &c.

KILKENNY.

218 3 17	343 10 0	309 14 0	235 16 0	The rent in this case is reduced at the sitting of the Court in

COUNTY.

5 0 10	uncertained,	4 12 2	4 19 2	
61 3 7	43 5 0	50 15 10	41 10 0	
132 0 22	53 6 0	65 0 0	62 0 0	
28 1 24	28 5 0	24 16 1	22 0 0	
17 0 7	11 5 0	12 3 9	13 3 8	
1 0 0	uncertained,	0 11 11	0 8 0	
19 2 0	14 15 0	15 19 8	16 0 0	
16 3 15	13 10 0	13 0 0	13 0 0	
19 3 17	9 10 0	15 0 0	9 0 0	And grazing of St. 2
59 0 9	21 0 0	13 16 0	21 0 0	
393 0 31	191 13 0	213 13 6	212 17 11	

MEATH.

IRISH LAND COMMISSION.

Names of Assistant Commissioners by whom Cases were decided.	No.	Name of Tenant.	Name of Landlord.	Townland.
Assistant Commissioners—				
W. F. BAILEY (Legal). R. BYRNE Q. W. TROTTER.	742	Catherine Noble,	Edward R. Taylor,	Newtown Oxley,
	743	Anne C. Oldcastle,	Earl of Fingall,	Kilshyer,
	744	John Kearney,	do.	Miltown & ants.,
	745	Stephen Ross-D,	Major General Sir H. P. Du Saha.	Cashel,
	746	Christopher Nulty,	Robert Taaffe and anor., avail. by John Taaffe and another.	Fargusstown,
	747	William N. Waller,	Edward Taylor,	Ballyboy,
	748	Richard S. V. Dyer, a taken, by Marcella A. E. Barrett and another.	Rev. Charles D. Scott,	Cushtown,
	749	Nicholas Gilsenan,	James McCann,	Tankardstown,
	750	Patrick Kane,	Lieut.-Col. J. N. Coddington,	Grange,
	751	Mrs. Mary Crabbie,	do.	do.
	752	William N. Waller,	do.	Fughto Hill,
	753	Hugh Kary,	John R. Coddington,	Nullamore,
				Total,

HEAD COMMISSIONER.	607	Mathew Connell,	Lord Greville,	Curraghmore,

HEAD COMMISSIONER.	1011	William Lacy,	William M. Glibbon,	Ankslog,
	1012	James Howell,	Count De Raymond,	Kilrunnagreen,
Assistant Commissioners—				
R. R. EADY (Legal). M. P. LYNCH. L. CHERRY.	1013	John Duff,	Earl of Portsmouth,	Kilcavanlea,
	1014	Richard Nannett,	do.	Claun,
	1015	William Waring,	do.	Killaley,
	1016	Patrick Fortune,	do.	do.
	1017	Arthur Rooke,	do.	Kilernagun,
	1018	Thomas Northwhale,	do.	do.
	1019	Do.	do.	do.
	1020	Patrick Fortune,	do.	do.
	1021	Anne Stephens,	do.	Tuumcollagh,
	1022	Nathaniel Stephens,	do.	Crannllagh,
				Total,

MEATH—*continued.*

Extent of Holding Acres.	Poor Law Valuation.	Former Rent.	Judicial Rent.	Observations.	Value of Tenancy.
A. R. P.	£ s. d.	£ s. d.	£ s. d.		£ s. d.
228 2 16	273 15 0	205 0 0	205 0 0		
162 3 39	197 10 0	260 15 8	207 10 0		
436 1 6	461 0 0	370 13 2	470 0 0		
115 3 33	132 0 0	130 0 0	115 0 0	By consent.	
58 0 0	67 10 0	86 8 7½	68 10 0		
52 0 6	60 0 0	64 0 0	62 10 0		
158 2 20	196 10 0	220 0 0	177 0 0		
70 1 33	85 10 0	135 5 6	90 0 0		
209 2 26	178 10 0	310 0 0	182 0 0		
52 2 2	57 10 0	68 0 0	56 0 0		
30 1 19	34 10 0	37 10 0	33 0 0		
14 1 18	14 5 0	17 0 0	13 0 0		
3,039 0 16	2,126 10 0	3,563 7 11½	2,104 0 0		

WESTMEATH.

Extent of Holding Acres.	Poor Law Valuation.	Former Rent.	Judicial Rent.	Observations.	Value of Tenancy.
10 0 26	7 10 0	6 0 0	5 0 0	The rent in this case was fixed by consent of the parties at the sitting of the Court in Dublin.	

WEXFORD.

Extent of Holding Acres.	Poor Law Valuation.	Former Rent.	Judicial Rent.	Observations.	Value of Tenancy.
12 0 6	6 5 0	5 0 0	7 0 0	The rent in this case was fixed by consent of the parties at the sitting of the Court in Dublin.	
119 2 11	68 0 0	76 1 0	80 0 0	do.	
97 0 11	76 0 0	83 0 0	65 0 0	By consent.	
87 3 10	66 13 0	64 17 0	50 0 0	do.	
112 3 16	64 10 0	76 0 0	60 16 0	do.	
35 0 0	10 0 0	12 10 0	10 10 0	do.	
77 0 23	unascertained.	85 5 0	61 16 0	do.	
141 0 0	do.	88 0 0	70 0 0	do.	
87 1 3	do.	16 0 0	19 0 0	do.	
16 0 37	do.	10 0 0	7 10 0	do.	
150 0 3	75 5 0	65 0 0	70 0 0	do.	
57 5 15	37 10 0	41 10 1	35 0 0	do.	
848 3 37	380 5 0	609 3 1	487 12 0		

IRISH LAND COMMISSION.

Names of Assistant Commissioners by whom Case was dealt.	No.	Name of Tenant.	Name of Landlord.	Townland.
Head Commission.	483	Robert Jones, ...	Sir Edward R. Hutchinson, Bart.	Kilshannon, ...

PROVINCE OF

Assistant Commissioners—				
B. R. Kane (Legal), G. R. Boyle, P. Callan.	367	Thomas Doyle, contd. in name of Patrick Doyle,	W. A. R. Umber and another, Trusts. of Christopher Umber.	Ballynacward, ...

Assistant Commissioners—				
W. F. Bailey (Legal), T. Davidson, T. A. Dillon.	320	Michael McGowan and another,	George L. Tottenham, ...	Aughaclish, —
	321	Patrick McGlain, senior,	do.	do. —
	322	Gilbert McGlain & anor., continued in name of Patrick McGlain.	do.	do. —
				Total —

Assistant Commissioners—				
W. F. Bailey (Legal), T. McCabe, L. W. Byrne.	628	Michael G. Sweeney, ...	Miss Harriett Dunham, contd. in the name of Mrs. Harriett Brown.	Calew and another,
	629	Pat Rafferty and two others,	Hercules R. Brabazon, —	Clonmore, —
	630	Winifred Lyons & anor.,	do.	do. —
	631	James Fitzgerald, ...	do.	do. —
	632	Pat Cormley, ...	do.	do. —
	633	Mary Rafferty, ...	do.	do. —
	634	Peter Rafferty and ors.,	do.	do. —
	635	Catherine Cunigan, ...	do.	do. —
	636	William Crealy & ors.,	do.	do. —
	637	Pat Cormien and others,	do.	do. —
				Total —

TABLE OF JUDICIAL RENTS.

WICKLOW.

Extent of Holding. Statute.	Poor Law Valuation.	Former Rent.	Judicial Rent.	Observations.
a. r. p.	£ s. d.	£ s. d.	£ s. d.	
98 0 5	37 0 0	40 0 0	30 0 0	The rent in this case was consent of the ju— sitting of the Court

CONNAUGHT.

GALWAY.

50 0 0	13 0 0	13 0 2	12 0 0	

LEITRIM.

23 1 2	4 0 0	3 10 0	5 0 0	
33 1 33	16 5 0	17 0 0	12 0 0	
28 3 31	18 10 0	21 0 0	18 16 0	
85 2 16	37 15 0	49 10 0	55 15 0	

ROSCOMMON.

PROVINCE OF

COUNTY OF

Names of Arbitrator Commissioners by whom Cases were decided.	No.	Name of Tenant.	Name of Landlord.	Townland.
HEAD COMMISSION.	1533	Jeremiah Ryan (John)	George Bolton, — —	Cromwell —

COUNTY OF

HEAD COMMISSION.	276	James Flaherty, —	Robert Cooke, — ...	Kilkenny, South

CIVIL BILL

PROVINCE OF

COUNTY OF

County Court Judge.	No.	Name of Tenant.	Name of Landlord.	Townland.
GEORGE WATERS, Q.C.			...	
	76	Patrick Wynn, ...	John D. Mahon & anor, ...	Drumrimm, —
	77	Mary Dolan, ...	Mrs Ellen Lannon, · ...	Cloughmagrillan,
	78	James Moran, ...	William C. D. O. Rathbone,	Stratormann, ...
	79	Thomas West & anor, ...	do.	Lissenularn, ...
	80	Mary Wynn & anor, ...	do.	do. —
	81	Michael Duggan, —	do. · · ...	Gubnigraish, ...
	82	Thomas Mahon & anor,	William Ready & others ...	Curraheugh ...
	83	Arthur Nicoll & anor, ...	do.	Gortnalenky, ...
	84	John M'Loughlin, —	do.	Cloudneugh, —
	85	Do. — ...	do.	Aranghbramlan,
				Total, ...

MUNSTER.

LIMERICK.

Extent of Holding, Statute.	Poor Law Valuation.	Former Rent.	Judicial Rent.	Observations.	Value of Tenancy.
A. R. P.	£ s. d.	£ s. d.	£ s. d.		£ s. d.
29 2 22	31 0 0	42 0 0	39 10 0	The rent in this case was fixed by consent of the parties at the sitting of the Court in Dublin.	

TIPPERARY.

| 54 1 0 | 50 15 0 | 57 0 0 | 45 0 0 | The rent in this case was fixed by consent of the parties at the sitting of the Court in Dublin. | |

COURTS.

CONNAUGHT.

LEITRIM.

Extent of Holding, Statute.	Poor Law Valuation.	Former Rent.	Judicial Rent.	Observations.	Value of Tenancy.
A. R. P.	£ s. d.	£ s. d.	£ s. d.		£ s. d.
29 0 21	10 7 0	9 10 0	8 0 0		
293 0 19	31 0 0	33 0 0	19 0 0		
9 0 7	3 15 0	3 19 0	2 15 0		
11 1 14	5 3 0	6 11 8	4 4 0		
11 1 14	5 0 0	6 16 0	4 4 0		
14 0 0	4 0 0	5 1 10	4 10 0		
7 3 23	5 6 0	5 10 0	3 0 0		
48 1 35	30 5 0	24 19 0	17 10 0		
11 1 6	4 6 0	6 10 0	3 10 0		
16 2 0	13 10 0	10 0 0	9 0 0		
451 2 11	105 12 0	107 17 4	73 14 0		

PROVINCE OF

COUNTY OF

County Court Judge	No.	Name of Tenant	Name of Landlord	Townland
J. G. Shaw, q.c.	140	John Commons, ...	Captain Thomas Glynn, ...	Knockanish, ...
	141	Mary Pierce, ...	Elizabeth H. Kitson, ...	Derry, ...
	142	Bartholomew Barry, ...	John R. F. Day, a Minor, by Sarah V. De Latour.	Ballinknockrane,
				Total, ...

COUNTY OF

T. A. Purcell, &c.	113	James Hurley, ...	Patrick Hurley, ...	Glenfield ...
	114	Peter Froghben, ...	La Marchesa Della Rosalia, ...	Dunmoylan and another.
	115	Patrick O'Shaughnessy,	do. ...	Kilmoury, ...
	116	James Kienahan, ...	do. ...	do. ...
				Total, ...

MUNSTER.

APRIL, 1892.

SUMMARIES FOR APRIL, 1892.

Summary showing, according to Provinces and Counties, the Number of Cases in which Judicial Rents have been Fixed by Sub-Commissions under the Land Law (Ireland) Act, 1881, during the Month of April, 1892; and also the Acreages, Tenement Valuations, Former Rents, and Judicial Rents of the Holdings.

Province and County.	No. of Cases in which Judicial Rents have been Fixed	Acreage.			Tenement Valuation.			Former Rent.			Judicial Rent.		
		Statute Acres.											
		A.	R.	P.	£	s.	d.	£	s.	d.	£	s.	d.
ULSTER—													
Antrim,	21	453	3	35	231	7	0	305	8	8	243	0	8
Donegal,	62	1,419	1	29	566	10	6	584	16	6	356	6	8
Fermanagh,	30	979	1	31	539	19	0	476	1	1	370	8	1
Total,	113	2,851	3	5	1,537	16	6	1,165	5	3	1,167	10	3
LEINSTER—													
Dublin,	16	719	0	12	707	10	0	1,111	1	21	809	13	0
Kilkenny,	110	4,657	3	9	2,826	19	0	3,364	13	9	2,076	16	8
King's,	1	215	0	17	110	5	0	110	0	0	90	0	0
Meath,	5	65	1	6	59	0	0	65	17	0	54	19	0
Queen's,	36	1,250	3	22	754	5	0	940	1	5	716	11	11
Wexford,	28	575	1	35	447	5	0	305	0	5	143	9	9
Total,	201	7,563	3	31	4,943	4	0	5,977	14	2	4,520	5	4
CONNAUGHT—													
Galway,	42	640	3	1	172	10	0	184	19	8	156	2	6
Leitrim,	14	213	3	20	105	4	0	115	13	6	87	5	0
Roscommon,	35	652	1	31	159	10	0	199	17	7	179	17	0
Total,	91	1,706	0	12	437	4	0	500	3	9	377	4	2
MUNSTER—													
Tipperary,	3	108	0	7	1	10	0	73	6	0	43	2	8

CIVIL BILL COURTS.

SUMMARY FOR APRIL, 1892.

Cases in which Judicial Rents have been fixed by Civil Bill Courts, under the Land Law (Ireland) Act, 1881, and notified to the Irish Land Commission during the Month of April, 1892.

Province and County.	Number of Cases in which Judicial Rents have been fixed.	Acreage.	Former Valuation.	Former Rent.	Judicial Rent.
		Statute Acres.			
		a. r. p.	£ s. d.	£ s. d.	£ s. d.
ULSTER—					
Cavan,	...	6	60 1 39	37 5 0	48 18 4	85 10 0
Donegal,	...	3	1,106 1 7	62 5 0	40 3 7	45 10 0
Totals,	...	8	1,166 2 39	99 10 0	88 15 11	78 6 0
LEINSTER—					
King's,	...	5	247 0 30	141 18 0	164 15 10	121 8 0
Meath,	...	5	37 5 18	22 0 0	32 4 0	25 6 0
Totals,	...	0	280 6 8	164 13 0	196 16 10	146 8 0
CONNAUGHT—					
Mayo,	...	16	180 3 18	79 10 0	94 5 10	79 11 0

IRELAND.

LEASEHOLDERS.

SUMMARY FOR APRIL, 1892.

Summary shewing, according to Provinces and Counties, the number of Cases in which Judicial Rents have been fixed by Chief and Sub-Commissioners, under the Land Law (Ireland) Act, 1887, during the Month of April, 1892, and also the Acreages, Tenement Valuations, Former Rents, and Judicial Rents of the Holdings.

Province and County.	Number of Cases in which Judicial Rents have been fixed.	Acreage.	Tenement Valuation.	Former Rent.	Judicial Rent.
		Statute Acres. A. R. P.	£ s. d.	£ s. d.	£ s. d.
ULSTER—					
Antrim, ...	7	303 2 1	168 8 6	190 12 0	157 1 6
Fermanagh, ...	4	213 1 38	176 5 0	153 16 6	123 16 6
Totals,	11	517 3 17	344 13 6	344 8 6	280 18 0
LEINSTER—					
Carlow, ...	3	80 0 12	—	88 15 6	76 1 0
Dublin, ...	10	207 0 28	870 5 0	695 1 7	476 0 0
Kilkenny, ...	18	1,631 2 36	815 5 0	1,117 3 8	863 2 0
Meath, ...	21	619 3 30	536 10 0	897 2 0	578 8 5
Queen's, ...	16	727 1 8	423 10 0	663 17 6	459 5 7
Wexford, ...	27	1,538 3 81	535 8 0	1,358 15 1	855 17 0
Totals,	94	4,834 3 13½	3,160 18 0	4,680 14 4	3,440 14 1
CONNAUGHT—					
Galway, ...	3	53 1 0	14 0 0	35 16 0	18 16 0
Roscommon, ...	2	146 2 2	123 10 0	116 13 6	99 0 0
Totals,	4	180 3 3	137 10 0	160 10 6	111 14 0
MUNSTER—					
Tipperary, ...	2	83 3 0	48 0 0	57 16 10	43 0 0

IRELAND.

ULSTER, —	11	517 3 17	344 13 6	344 8 6	280 18 0
LEINSTER, —	94	4,834 3 13½	3,180 18 0	4,680 14 4	3,440 14 1
CONNAUGHT, ...	4	180 3 3	137 10 0	160 10 6	111 14 0
MUNSTER, ...	2	83 3 0	48 0 0	57 16 10	43 0 0
TOTALS ...	111	5,617 1 13½	3,711 1 6	5,043 10 3	3,876 6 1

CIVIL BILL COURTS.

LEASEHOLDERS.

SUMMARY FOR APRIL, 1892.

Cases in which Judicial Rents have been fixed by the Civil Bill Courts under the Land Law (Ireland) Act, 1887, and notified to the Irish Land Commission during the Month of April, 1892.

Parishes and County.	Number of Cases in which Judicial Rents have been Fixed.	Arrears.	Poor-law Valuation.	Former Rent.	Judicial Rent.
		Statute Acre. A. R. P.	£ s. d.	£ s. d.	£ s. d.
ULSTER—					
Cavan, ...	11	143 3 29	91 18 0	93 8 7	70 10 6
Donegal, ...	1	63 3 20	28 0 0	35 0 0	28 0 0
Totals, ...	12	207 3 9	119 18 0	127 8 7	98 10 6
CONNAUGHT—					
Mayo, ...	1	4 3 17	—	3 0 0	8 0 0
MUNSTER—					
Cork, ...	1	137 3 0	127 3 0	140 0 0	103 0 0

IRELAND.

ULSTER, ...	12	207 3 9	119 18 0	127 8 7	98 10 6
CONNAUGHT, ...	1	4 3 17	—	8 0 0	2 0 0
MUNSTER, ...	1	137 3 0	127 5 0	140 0 0	103 0 0
TOTALS, ...	14	350 0 26	247 8 0	269 8 7	203 10 6

PROVINCE OF

COUNTY OF

Names of Assistant Commissioners by whom Case was decided	No.	Name of Tenant	Name of Landlord	Townland
R. Owens (Legal). A. R. Montgomery, R. Johnston.	4413	James Allen,	John A. Arnott and another, Trustees of V. A. St. M. Shiel,	O'Hara's,
	4424	Jane Duffin,	do.	Aingh'l,
	4427	Robert Dysart,	Lieutenant Ferguson,	Coolybracken,
	4428	James O. Fullerton,	Samuel Thompson,	Ballyclunentin,
	4429	Adam Hamilton,	Alexander McMaster, Exor., of James Moorehead,	Tully,
	4430	Robert Boune,	do.	do.
	4431	Margaret O. Topping,	William Saunderson,	Sherry Wherry,
	4432	Thomas Lamont & mor.,	J. B. Whitfield and others,	Greenhill,
	4433	William Blaney,	Mary A. O'Hara and another,	Linnary,
	4434	Alexander Miller,	Colonel McDonald,	Brackley,
	4435	John Mitchell,	John Greene,	Carnmacon,
	4436	Hugh McBride,	John B. Dunlop,	Aghaleek,
	4437	William McCurdy,	do.	Crumplmort,
	4438	Robert Gray,	Colonel Edmund Leslie,	Kilmoyle,
	4439	John O'Hare,	H. McC. McGildowney, Committee of Charles McGildowney, a lunatic,	Toriff,
	4440	Francis Black, senior & another,	Lord Antrim,	Kilmure,
	4441	Kate Money and another,	do.	do.
	4442	Daniel Black,	George W. Coppage, & another, Trustees of Alex. Coppage,	Turnaghnany,
	4443	Catherine McClambridge,	John Turnley,	Clochmahill,
	4444	Do.	do.	do.
	4445	John McBride,	do.	Faughill,
				Total,

COUNTY OF

Assistant Commissioners—	4652	Elias McAward,	Robert O. Montgomery,	Printown,
R. Owens (Legal). R. Rogers. J. Bane.	4653	Samuel Taylor,	James B. Delap,	Drummaness,
	4654	Mathew Fairman,	John Graham,	Tulnamallen,

ULSTER.

ANTRIM.

Name of Holding. Statute.	Poor Law Valuation.	Former Rent.	Judicial Rent.	Observations.	Value of Tenancy.
A. R. P.	£ s. d.	£ s. d.	£ s. d.		£ s. d.
10 1 10	6 5 0	7 4 0	6 4 0		
10 0 38	13 10 0	7 10 0	7 10 0		
33 2 0	13 10 0	11 8 0	11 10 0	With right of grazing over 484. in 80P.	
9 0 10	9 16 0	9 0 8	7 3 0		
8 1 51	uncertained,	8 0 0	3 10 0		
10 1 28	do.	9 10 0	8 16 0		
34 0 34	12 5 0	16 0 0	18 0 0		
58 1 10	85 0 0	65 0 0	33 0 0	By consent.	
17 3 84	13 10 0	17 0 0	16 0 0		
44 6 20	40 5 0	44 5 0	33 0 0		
77 3 83	uncertained,	8 10 0	8 8 0		
23 0 6	13 7 0	13 17 3	9 0 0		
29 0 10	14 10 0	11 0 0	9 0 0		
16 3 27	11 18 0	10 16 2	8 12 0		
71 2 33	17 0 0	18 18 4	16 0 0	And two acres grazing on mountain.	
31 0 0	18 10 0	11 4 10	10 8 0		
44 3 5	uncertained,	54 19 6	24 18 8		
1 0 20	do.	1 10 0	0 16 0		
5 3 28	8 5 0	8 0 0	8 0 0		
18 0 5	13 10 0	19 15 6	18 4 0		
4 0 0	4 10 0	4 17 4	4 0 0		
452 5 35	631 7 0	305 6 8	246 0 8		

DONEGAL.

Name of Assistant Commissioners by whom Cases were decided.	No.	Name of Tenant.	Name of Landlord.	Townland.
Assistant Commissioners—				
R. Green (Legal.)	6685	Daniel McGranaghan, —	Marquis Conyngham,	Hornmoulm,
H. Somervale.	6686	William Crown, Limited admr. of Mary Crown.	John Taylor,	Creggan,
J. Kirk.	6687	Ross Hastings,	Col. C. H. Knox, —	Narray,
	6688	Thomas Quinn, —	do.	Ballyhalry,
	6689	Jane McGranagle, —	Robert Stuart, —	Doulsk,
	6690	Michael McGroarty, —	Joseph Kerrigan,	Mournemullin,
	6691	Eliza J. Cathers,	Mrs. Harriette Harrison,	Doolsk,
	6692	George Patton,	Sir Samuel Hayes, Bt., and ors.	do.
	6693	John McDaid,	James Griffith,	do.
	6694	Samuel Gregory,	Henry Bruen Junr., Trustees of Thomas Conolly.	Mullen,
	6695	Henry McClure,	Col R. G. Montgomery,	Maghanappple,
	6696	Charles M'Ginty,	do.	Tumboloy,
	6697	Samuel Gilchrist,	do.	Mournemullin,
	6698	William J. McClure,	do.	Maghanappple,
	6699	Alexander Ferron,	do.	Milford & ors.
	6700	Samuel Maxwell,	John Cochrane,	Tremanellan,
	6701	Francis Kelly,	Viscount Lifford,	Goland,
	6702	Scott Snodgrass,	James R. Dukes,	Drumfergus,
	6703	Neal Elliral, —	do.	do.
	6704	Hugh Taylor,	do.	Drumineson,
	6705	Eliza J. Cathers,	Lady Chichester,	Doolsk,
	6706	John McBride, Dep. of Anne McBride.	do.	do.
	6707	William McBride,	do.	do.
	6708	Edward McManama, —	do.	do.
	6709	Eliza Magee,	Charles H. Knox,	Ballyhalry,
	6710	Do.	do.	do.
	6711	Do.	do.	do.
	6712	Do.	do.	do.
	6713	John McBrearty,	Charles Johnston, unstamped in name of C. J. Johnston, a minor, and others.	Carralew,
	6714	Michael McBrearty,	do.	do.
	6715	John McBrearty (Michael)	do.	do.
	6716	Bridget Bradley, Limited Admix. of John Bradley, junior.	do.	do.
	6717	Daniel McManama,	do.	do.
	6718	John McBrearty,	do.	do.

DONEGAL—*continued.*

Extent of Holding. Statute.	Poor Law Valuation.	Former Rent.	Judicial Rent.	Observations.
A. R. P.	£ s. d.	£ s. d.	£ s. d.	
5 3 14	13 0 0	17 1 8	18 0 0	
1 3 20	1 0 0	1 10 0	1 0 0	
3 3 20	unascertained,	5 15 0	4 4 0	
4 3 15	3 5 0	3 3 0	3 5 0	
10 0 35	7 5 0	3 4 0	3 14 0	
73 0 34	4 10 0	6 6 0	5 12 0	
3 1 15	unascertained,	0 15 0	0 7 0	
48 1 30	22 0 0	22 7 0	17 0 0	
30 3 20	8 0 0	4 4 0	8 7 8	
20 1 20	11 0 0	13 6 0	11 10 0	
51 1 35	38 5 0	46 15 6	43 10 0	
10 0 0	5 10 0	6 11 0	4 5 0	
11 3 15	10 10 6	13 17 3	10 5 0	
34 3 29	21 0 0	22 5 5	16 0 0	
14 1 5	12 10 0	13 9 9	8 0 0	
39 3 10	24 10 0	28 0 0	23 10 0	
14 2 32	4 19 0	5 10 0	4 0 0	
87 0 0	40 0 0	40 14 0	35 0 0	
60 0 34	22 0 4	30 19 10	26 0 0	
40 3 20	31 10 0	31 17 8	37 0 0	
6 0 35	2 0 0	2 14 6	3 5 0	
1 3 0	2 0 0	1 15 0	1 9 0	
6 2 20	3 5 0	3 15 0	2 15 0	
13 2 0	2 10 0	3 10 0	2 17 6	
3 0 20	unascertained,	14 13 0	10 10 0	
2 3 30	unascertained,	5 0 0	3 7 0	
3 1 15	unascertained,	8 0 0	3 15 0	
0 2 35	unascertained,	11 0 0	0 10 0	
6 3 34	2 17 9	4 16 3	3 0 0	
15 3 20	3 19 0	4 15 0	8 10 0	
10 2 13	2 10 0	1 10 0	3 3 0	
7 3 3	8 15 0	3 12 1½	3 10 0	
49 1 14	7 5 0	6 3 3½	5 0 0	
13 3 25	4 0 0	6 19 6	4 5 0	

Names of Assistant Commissioners by whom Cases were decided.	No.	Name of Tenant.	Name of Landlord.	Townland.
Assistant Commissioners— E. Cross (Legal) R. Stovell. J. Ross.	6719	Daniel M'Crohire, ...	Charles Johnston, contd. in name of C. J. Johnston, a Minor, and others.	Carrolan, ...
	6720	Catherine McMenamin,	do.	do. ...
	6721	John Doherty, ...	do.	do. ...
	6722	Ellen J. Cathers, ...	Sir Samuel H. Hayes, Bart.,	Mullanaghran, ...
	6723	Margaret Gallaugh, ...	do.	Cappry, ...
	6724	Ellen Walsh, ...	do. — —	do. ...
	6725	Rodger Dufley, ...	do.	do. ...
	6726	Sarah Ramsey, ...	do. — —	Doolah, ...
	6727	John Lawn, ...	do.	Cappry, ...
	6728	John McCormick, ...	do.	Meenmurrigach, ...
	6729	Maurice Gallan, ...	do. — —	Doolah, ...
	6730	Thomas McCormick, ...	do. — ...	Meenacurrigach, ...
	6731	John McBride, ...	do. — ...	Doolah, ...
	6732	William Roe, ...	do. — ...	Cappry, ...
	6733	James Lerper, ...	do. — —	Drumboe, ...
	6734	John Morrow, ...	do. — —	Liskervan, ...
	6735	William Dinsmore, ...	do. ... —	do. ...
	6736	Jeremiah Bonar, ...	do. — —	do. ...
	6737	Patrick Kerrigan, ...	do. — ...	Lettermore, ...
	6738	James Oliver, ...	do. — ...	Callan, ...
	6739	Darby McCloud, ...	do. — —	Stranagibbath, ...
	6740	Hugh McGabbrick, ...	do. — ...	do. ...
	6741	Joseph McGonagle, ...	do. ... —	Mullanaghran, ...
	6742	Francis Given, ...	do. — —	do. ...
	6743	Richard Magee, ...	do.	Cappry, ...
				Total, ...

DONEGAL—*continued.*

Extent of Holding. Acres.	Poor Law Valuation.	Former Rent.	Judicial Rent.	Observations.	Value of Tenancy.
£ s. p.	£ s. d.	£ s. d.	£ s. d.		£ s. d.
11 1 5	4 10 0	4 4 9	3 15 0		
36 1 27	5 0 0	6 3 3	4 8 0		
87 2 39	5 15 0	5 14 0	4 12 0		
13 3 24	7 5 0	7 0 0	5 10 0		
23 1 27	13 0 0	14 15 0	10 15 0		
14 1 15	4 0 0	5 3 0	4 8 0		
13 3 32	5 5 0	5 13 0	5 17 0		
10 0 34	7 0 0	5 0 0	5 10 0		
6 1 35	3 10 0	3 16 0	2 0 0		
10 3 23	unascertained.	5 10 0	3 14 0	And 6a. 1r. 39p. undivided mountain.	
8 2 50	3 0 0	3 6 0	5 10 0		
4 0 20	3 5 0	3 3 6	2 3 0	And ½ of 30a. 0r. 25p. undivided mountain.	
14 0 38	4 5 0	4 13 0	3 15 0		
16 1 8	4 0 0	7 5 0	5 5 0		
13 0 45	8 10 0	10 0 0	7 16 0		
105 0 15	unascertained.	16 0 0	14 0 0		
13 3 30	3 10 0	8 0 0	3 12 0		
20 2 30	4 8 0	6 0 0	4 5 0		
14 1 0	4 15 0	6 0 0	4 15 0		
18 3 10	11 16 0	13 0 0	9 10 0		
20 2 45	7 10 0	7 10 0	6 10 0		
15 1 25	4 10 0	5 3 0	5 0 0		
22 3 0	7 0 0	8 10 0	4 15 0		
46 3 25	13 0 0	13 15 0	11 5 0		
40 1 30	33 0 0	33 10 10	26 0 0		
1,117 1 13	646 10 6	664 15 6	528 4 6		

FERMANAGH.

Names of Assistant Commissioners by whom Court was decided.	No.	Name of Tenant.	Name of Landlord.	Townland.
Assistant Commissioners—				
W. F. Bailey (Legal). T. A. Dickson. T. Davison.	2263	Mary Murray,	Earl of Arran,	Carrickliss,
	2270	John McHOuguer,	do.	Gorman,
	2271	John Downey,	do.	Milltown.
	2272	Thomas Magovren,	do.	Derryiss,
	2273	James McCelroy,	do.	do.
	2274	Andrew McKenna,	do.	do.
	2275	Patrick Erskine, senior and junior.	do.	Drumersult,
	2276	John Gilroy,	do.	do.
	2277	John Moffat, sued in names of Rev. John McKnight and Richard J. Hovn.	do.	Shantavbla,
	2278	John Moffat, sued in room of George Moffat.	do.	Molly,
	2279	Emily Graham,	do.	Claryturkle,
	2280	Hugh McAvenny,	do.	Farmall,
	2281	John Rogers,	do.	do.
	2282	William Bullock,	do.	Aghalane,
	2283	William John Miskn,	do.	Currabrush and another.
	2284	George Fleming,	do.	Derrychrin,
	2285	Alexander Ross,	do.	Derrycassan,
	2286	James Johnson,	do.	Tattry,
	2287	Archibald Foble,	Mrs. R. James and others,	Coolhill,
	2288	Catherine McCormick,	Francis A. Johnston,	Drumgallon,
	2289	Michael McElgunn,	Alexander Maguire,	Naan Island,
	2290	John Graham,	The Misses May Mayne, Ada Mayne, Rebel Mayne, and M. E. Ormsby.	Mount Derby,
	2291	Peter Maguire,	Dr. R. Collum and W. N. Collum.	Carrogain,
	2292	James Maguire,	do.	do.
E. Green (Legal) J. J. Oxley. R. Johnston	2293	Andrew Murphy, junior,	Earl of Enniskillen,	Crocknacrooy,
				Total,

FERMANAGH—continued.

Extent of Holding. Statute.	Poor Law Valuation.	Former Rent.	Judicial Rent.	Observations.	Value of Tenancy.
a. r. p.	£ s. d.	£ s. d.	£ s. d.		£ s. d.
26 1 30	10 10 0	9 6 0	7 7 0		
25 0 65	13 0 0	11 0 0	9 0 0		
14 3 0	9 5 0	7 12 0	6 10 0		
19 0 10	7 5 0	6 13 0	5 0 0		
36 0 0	14 5 0	10 0 0	8 5 0		
17 1 13	9 15 0	6 17 0	5 6 0		
23 1 25	15 0 0	11 0 0	9 10 0		
8 0 30	6 15 0	4 15 0	4 0 0		
43 0 05	23 10 0	21 0 0	20 0 0		
34 2 15	16 5 0	15 5 0	13 13 0		
21 1 15	9 5 0	9 0 0	7 6 0		
60 0 0	15 9 0	15 8 0	12 10 0		
35 0 20	23 3 0	10 4 0	15 0 0		
115 0 30	75 0 0	76 1 9	75 1 9		
64 3 32	33 10 0	27 14 0	21 0 0		
66 2 30	57 16 0	57 0 0	77 10 0		
33 1 25	19 5 0	17 0 0	13 15 0		
23 1 0	24 15 0	21 6 0	17 17 0		
43 0 0	8 5 0	7 10 0	6 15 0		
13 3 5	15 0 0	12 0 0	10 0 0		
43 0 10	20 0 0	23 15 4	17 15 0		
38 1 20	17 0 0	15 3 0	12 0 0		
13 0 0	4 15 0	5 0 0	4 10 0		
15 2 33	5 5 0	5 0 0	4 15 0		

IRISH LAND COMMISSION.

PROVINCE OF

COUNTY OF

Name of Assistant Commissioners by whom Cases were decided.	No.	Name of Tenant.	Name of Landlord.	Townland.
Assistant Commissioners—				
R. R. KANE (Legal). J. HACONTON. A. N. COMER.	436	Bernard Lloyd, ...	Richard Nolan, continued in name of A. Ross and another.	Newbank, ...
	437	Michael Laughlin, ...	Charlotte M. Perkinson, ...	Kilalawn, ...
	438	John Boothman, ...	Edward H. Webb and another, continued by Mary A. Boothman and another.	Drougal, ...
	439	Michael Flanagan, ...	Joseph Flood, ...	Golden Bridge, &.,
	440	John Molloy, ...	James F. Duncan, ...	do. ...
	441	William Taylor, ...	Lord Massy, ...	Woodtown, ...
	442	Patrick Mowney, ...	Captain Robert Smith & anor.,	Crumlin, ...
	443	William Lockridge, ...	Patrick Dunne, ...	Ashfield, ...
	444	Do., ...	Right Hon. Ion T. Hamilton,	do. ...
	445	Thomas McUnistace, ...	Sylvester R. Kerr, ...	Commons of Ratoath, &c.,
	446	Maria Mortimer, ...	John Wills, ...	Belgardly, ...
	447	Anne Butler, ...	John H. Burton, ...	Cloudelkin, ...
	448	James Dowling, ...	do.	Bedford St, ...
	449	Mary Anne Poynton, ...	John Bathurst, contd. in name of Mary A. Boothman & anor.	Castle Bankov, ...
	450	Edward Carthy, ...	Earl of Mealford and others, ...	Mount Pelier and another.
	451	William Dowling, ...	William F. Smith, ...	Yellow Meadows,
	452	Terence Murphy, ...	Mrs. Mary A. Fox, Commissioner of Sir Compton Domville.	Ballyfermot, Upr.,
	453	Michael Mahon, ...	Joseph P. Tyndall, ...	Kilmardan, ...
			Total, ...	

COUNTY OF

Assistant Commissioners—				
L. DOYLE (Legal). W. WALPOLE. C. O'KEEFFE.	2371	John Lynch, ...	Rev. John W. Bell, ...	Knockbregh, ...
	3373	John Phelan, ...	do.	do. ...
	2373	Michael Stapleton, ...	do.	do. ...
	2374	John Lynch, continued in name of William Lynch,	Silver C. Oliver and others, ...	Mallardstown, Lr.,
	2375	Michael Norris, ...	Richard M. Rennie, ...	Kilmancard, Lower,
	2376	Thomas Larkin, ...	Michael Norris, ...	Castrellstown and another,
	2377	Nicholas Leamby, ...	Joseph Galloway, surviving Trustee of John Andrews.	Ballygown Roads,
	2378	Peter Hinkey, ...	John Andrews and another,	do. ...
	2379	Michael Dunne, ...	Viscount Mountgarrett, ...	Gombrimgarden,
	2380	James Hayden, ...	do.	Loughnafish, ...

LEINSTER.

DUBLIN.

Extent of Holding Statute.	Poor Law Valuation.	Former Rent.	Judicial Rent.	Observations.	Value of Tenancy.
a. r. p.	£ s. d.	£ s. d.	£ s. d.		£ s. d.
53 0 6	unascertained,	149 0 0	104 0 0		
41 1 35	89 10 0	60 17 10	49 0 0		
19 3 33	16 0 0	24 8 0	30 0 0		
6 1 0	14 0 0	32 0 0	89 0 0		
15 0 22	35 10 0	64 8 0	43 0 0		
818 3 30	857 10 0	357 8 8	775 0 0		
25 3 18	65 15 0	100 0 0	79 10 0		
6 8 24	20 0 0	18 0 0	11 8 0		
5 0 16	6 10 0	8 9 3	8 15 0		
6 1 14	5 10 0	8 2 6	6 5 0		
23 1 15	64 0 0	49 0 0	87 10 0		
5 0 4	8 0 0	13 18 4	10 15 0		
5 3 15	13 10 0	13 0 0	8 0 0		
61 3 17	106 0 0	136 18 5	114 0 0		
213 0 13	45 5 0	43 8 0	48 0 0		
4 1 20	6 10 0	9 9 0	8 13 0		
20 1 63	32 0 0	83 2 0	61 0 0		
2 0 0	unascertained,	4 0 0	8 0 0		
719 0 12	797 10 0	1,141 1 11	906 13 0		

KILKENNY.

66 3 3	42 0 0	47 0 0	34 7 6		
40 3 8	83 0 0	25 0 0	18 15 0		
16 1 16	13 3 6	15 10 0	6 6 3		
4 3 17	8 0 0	5 0 0	8 0 6		

Name of Assistant Commissioners by whom Case was decided.	No.	Name of Tenant.	Name of Landlord.	Townland.
Assistant Commissioners—				
L. North (Legal).	2381	Richard Bruckshaw, ...	Mrs. F. M. Johnston, coptd. in estate of Chpd. R. C. Kent,	Usherdale,
W. Walpole.	2382	Michael Duggan,	Orland Villiers Stuart, ...	Harbordsde,
C. O'Keeffe.	2383	John Hayes,	do. ...	do.
	2384	Daniel J. Stephens,	Vincent Ashbrook, ...	Tullamain,
	2385	Allen Keefe,	Edward M. Twomey,	Kilvet and anor.
	2386	Patrick Mullins,	Mark Bradley, ..	Gortyvangan Lo.
	2387	James Brennan,	James Murphy, ..	Rathduff,
	2388	James Moore,	Osband J. Marsh,	Brookstown,
	2389	Martin Lynch,	Robert Neville and another,	Ahenure,
	2390	Thomas Luttrell,	do.	Ahenure North,
	2391	Margaret Cantwell,	Rev. Alexander King and ors.	Rockin,
	2392	Walter Shea,	do. ...	do.
	2393	Edward Comerford,	do.	do.
	2394	Margaret Leahy,	do.	do.
	2395	Patrick Crowley,	Florence O'Brien,	Mullinary,
	2396	Do.	do.	Shalis,
	2397	William Wall,	do.	Foulkrath and another,
	2398	Do.	do.	do.
	2399	John Morris,	do.	Monmarsh,
	2400	Do.	do.	Mulinary and ors.
	2401	Do.	do.	Whiteland,

KILKENNY—continued.

Extent of Holding. Statute.	Post Law Valuation	Former Rent.	Judicial Rent.	Observations.	Term of Tenancy.
a. r. p	£ s. d	£ s. d.	£ s. d.		£ s. d.
11 3 12	13 0 0	11 7 8	11 7 8		
52 1 30	32 10 0	32 0 0	23 7 4		
111 1 39	112 15 0	130 0 0	87 0 0		
51 3 0	11 10 0	50 0 0	42 0 0		
159 2 30	155 0 0	162 14 8	200 17 8		
9 3 15	unconrectioned,	14 0 0	1 7 6		
76 3 34	16 10 0	16 10 0	13 10 1		
243 1 7	150 10 0	170 0 0	140 0 0		
7 3 34	unconsidered,	3 0 7	3 0 7		
11 0 4	8 5 0	9 18 0	6 17 6		
60 1 19	40 0 0	34 0 0	33 0 0		
116 0 31	71 0 0	66 10 0	85 10 0		
89 3 29	63 0 0	51 10 0	39 10 0		
60 1 16	42 10 0	34 0 0	31 0 4		
4 1 1	10 0 0	11 6 3	9 0 0		
16 2 25	11 10 0	11 4 8	11 5 0		
36 3 14	34 10 0	87 3 11	97 10 0		
6 0 20	5 5 0	6 9 6	6 4 8		
91 1 23	13 15 0	16 10 0	10 10 0		
61 2 20	31 0 0	33 11 0	27 7 8		
2 1 25	1 15 0	1 17 0	1 4 0		
33 1 39	18 5 0	18 10 0	14 15 0		
71 3 30	21 16 0	36 0 0	22 0 0		
118 0 23	52 10 0	51 0 0	44 10 0		
34 0 3	11 0 0	16 10 0	11 0 0		
90 2 33	41 0 0	61 5 0	63 13 0		
13 0 30	7 0 0	7 0 0	6 0 0		
89 1 17	67 5 0	77 17 8	45 0 0		
11 1 14	7 0 0	7 10 6	6 15 0		
11 1 25	9 10 0	10 6 0	7 16 0		
8 1 0	3 0 0	1 10 0	1 0 0		
6 3 20	6 0 0	6 10 0	6 0 0		
9 1 23	6 0 0	9 0 0	7 3 0		

Names of Assistant Commissioners by whom Cases were decided.	No.	Name of Tenant	Name of Landlord
Assistant Commissioners— L. Doyle. E. H. Bayly. R. Gilliland.	8514	Thomas White,	... Col. F. B. B. Tighe, trustee of E. K. Tighe
	8515	Robert Ison,	... Mrs. Emily Tweedy,

Extent of Holding, Townlands	Poor Law Valuation.			Former Rent.			Judicial Rent.		
A. R. P.	£	s.	d.	£	s.	d.	£	s.	d.
36 0 2	33	0	0	23	0	0	16	0	0
147 3 18	40	0	0	108	10	0	87	0	0
31 2 31	13	10	0	18	0	0	14	16	0
13 1 31	14	5	0	16	12	2	11	0	8
20 3 1	15	15	0	15	11	0	13	0	0
57 3 17	24	0	0	23	0	0	21	7	4
31 3 15	11	0	0	16	0	0	10	15	0
8 0 33	5	0	0	5	5	0	4	10	0
10 2 0	untenanted,			2	0	0	1	13	4
31 3 25	4	15	0	8	10	0	5	7	6
34 0 34	15	15	0	11	0	0	11	12	4
38 1 34	17	5	0	13	0	10	15	4	10
19 1 30	10	0	0	8	10	5	8	10	8
31 1 6	untenanted,			86	14	8	34	10	0
301 1 11	197	5	0	155	16	8	106	0	0
32 2 37	28	5	0	31	16	0	38	4	0
33 3 34	13	0	0	18	0	0	10	15	0
10 5 4	6	15	0	5	0	6	2	10	0
8 1 8	3	0	0	1	4	8	3	12	8
16 3 36	7	0	0	6	12	0	8	3	6
11 3 11	13	5	0	12	16	6	9	10	0
61 0 26	30	5	0	31	17	0	26	5	0
25 3 10	17	0	0	18	11	10	12	0	0
13 2 14	8	0	0	6	0	0	6	17	8
13 0 17	5	5	0	10	0	5	8	5	0
20 1 31	14	15	0	16	3	2	13	7	6
26 0 0	8	5	0	11	9	6	4	10	0
24 1 37	10	15	0	13	15	5	6	10	0
1 3 30	1	10	0	3	5	0	1	10	0
18 1 26	23	0	0	27	3	6	20	15	0
7 1 5	3	10	6	6	0	9	8	17	6
33 0 34	18	10	0	16	0	0	13	10	0
133 0 4	105	0	0	108	0	0	80	0	0
44 3 11	18	6	0	25	0	0	23	6	0
65 2 37	31	0	0	31	0	0	17	17	6

Names of Assistant Commissioners by whom Cases were settled	No.	Name of Tenant.	Name of Landlord.	Townland.
Assistant Commissioners—				
L. Dures (Legal).	2449	James Maher,	Elizabeth G. Davis,	Ballyredddy,
R. R. Bayly.	2450	Patrick Scahan,	Sir J. Coghill, Bart.,	Millicen,
R. Gawland.	2451	Patrick Purcell,	do.	Ballylaycy,
	2452	Patrick Treld,	do.	Park,
	2453	Richard Hennessy,	do.	Griffinstown,
	2454	Michael Murphy,	do.	Blackally,
	2455	Daniel White,	do.	Kilkitran,
	2456	John Bergin,	Earl of Clonmel,	Garbrunerbeal,
	2457	William Dunne, Ltd. Administ. of Bridget Purcell,	do.	do.
	2458	Patrick Dunne,	do.	do.
	2459	John Carroll,	do.	do.
	2460	John Shee,	do.	do.
	2461	Stephen Brannigan,	do.	do.
	2462	Mary Delany,	do.	do.
	2463	Patrick Watson,	do.	do.
	2464	Thomas Walsh,	Peter W. Henrian, a minor, by Catherine A. Henrian & others,	Castleen,
	2465	James Mahon,	do.	do.
	2466	William Nolan,	do.	do.
	2467	Michael Walsh,	do.	do.
	2468	Do.	do.	do.
	2469	Patrick Murphy,	do.	do.
	2470	James Kaughan,	A. M. Kavanagh, devisee in issue of W. Kavanagh.	Timbrien,
	2471	Charles Kennedy,	do.	Rannahowen,
	2472	Cornelius Phelan,	do.	Sraleigh & same,
	2473	Do.	do.	do.
	2474	James Shannon,	do.	Oode,
	2475	Do.	do.	Ballynaloshan,
	2476	Martin Phelan,	do.	Rannahowen,
	2477	Michael Dewary,	do.	Dunaghmore,
	2478	James Purcell,	do.	Stamthtown,
	2479	Do.	do.	do.
	2480	John Murphy,	do.	Monte,
				Total,

KILKENNY—*continued.*

Extent of Holding. Statute.			Poor Law Valuation.			Former Rent.			Judicial Rent.		
A.	R.	P.	£	s.	d.	£	s.	d.	£	s.	d.
45	1	0	60	5	6	84	10	0	23	10	0
17	0	6	18	0	0	13	2	6	9	5	0
90	3	15	89	0	0	32	0	0	26	13	6
16	1	13	6	5	0	6	10	0	5	5	0
41	3	34	17	0	0	20	1	0	14	10	0
17	0	0	7	15	0	10	13	6	4	10	6
100	0	69	56	0	0	45	0	0	45	0	0
20	0	6	20	0	0	23	14	3	17	0	0
6	1	21	4	5	9	6	0	0	3	6	0
1	2	23	1	15	0	1	10	6	1	6	6
14	0	6	11	0	0	10	6	0	9	3	6
65	0	31	19	10	0	20	11	0	16	5	0
52	2	65	22	15	0	23	17	4	15	15	0
3	3	5	4	0	0	3	4	0	2	15	0
7	1	6	6	0	0	6	17	3	4	3	6
6	2	14	3	15	0	6	0	0	3	15	0
16	3	13	6	0	0	7	1	6	6	0	0
52	3	0	20	0	0	20	8	4	16	10	0
43	0	3	16	16	6	31	15	0	17	4	6
6	3	77	6	10	0	6	6	6	6	15	0
60	1	6	23	6	0	26	9	0	22	6	0
31	2	31	23	0	0	22	5	3	18	18	0
10	2	12	13	0	0	13	16	6	11	6	0
143	2	31	124	0	0	123	13	3	104	6	0
6	5	0	6	15	0	6	6	6	7	10	6
64	2	6	50	10	0	42	6	6	37	0	0
71	0	20	47	13	0	46	13	6	41	10	0

KING'S

Names of Assistant Commissioners by whom Cases were decided.	No.	Name of Tenant.	Name of Landlord.	Townland.
Assistant Commissioners— R. R. Kane (Legal). J. Haughton. A. N. Crofte.	1920	Patrick Murtagh, ...	Mary Tyrrell, ...	Clonmacnoise and another.

COUNTY OF

Assistant Commissioners— W. F. Bailey (Legal). S. Byrne. G. N. Thompson	1692	Patrick McDonnell, ...	Charles W. Osborne,	Rummers, ...
	1693	Catherine Nelson, ...	Rev. G. B. Martin, ...	Ballynahinch, —
	1694	Philip Smith, —	do. —	Balrath, ...
	1695	Anne Carpenter, ...	Sir Henry P. De Bathe, ...	Knightstown, —
	1696	Mary Jones, —	do. —	do. ...
				Total, —

QUEEN'S

Assistant Commissioners— L. Doyle (Legal). J. MacKenzie. G. W. Thompson.	1897	Anne M. Jackson, —	Viscount de Vesci,	Blackhills, ...
	1898	Martin Bergin, —	Mrs. P. Grattan Bellew,	Ballygorhan, Upr.,
	1899	John Keating, —	George Butts, ...	Ballybrittas, —
Assistant Commissioners— L. Doyle (Legal). J. McKenna. J. Patterson.	1900	Edward Laker, —	Viscount de Vesci,	Crossbarns, —
	1901	Anne M. Jackson, —	do. —	Tullyroe, —
	1902	Nathaniel Oxley, —	Lord Castletown, ...	Coolkerry, —
	1903	John Ennis, ...	Rev. John H. Warnford, ...	Ballymullen, ...
	1904	Henry Mitchell, —	R. H. Sankies. ...	Clonmore, —
	1905	Richard Orange, —	do. ...	Clonmore & another,
	1906	Charles Champ, ...	Maxwell G. Close,	Dublin-sleigh and others,
	1907	Bridget Kehoe, ...	Colonel R. G. Crosby,	Knocklesh, ...
	1908	Martin Dowling, ...	do. —	Fossy, Upper and another,
	1909	Oliver Murphy, —	do. —	Fossy, Upper, ...
	1910	Michael McDonnell, —	do. ...	do. ...
	1911	James McCormack, ...	do. ...	do. ...
	1912	Mary Egan, ...	Major W. Floran, continued in names of N. de N. Floran, a lunatic, by E. A. Wylundrick and William G. Townsend, his Committees.	Kilcrannis, ...
	1913	Martin Delaney, ...	Guardians of J. H. W. Shane and W. P. C. Shane.	Cappacumlaghy, ...

COUNTY.

Extent of Holding. Statute.	Poor Law Valuation.	Former Rent.	Judicial Rent.	Observations.	Value of Tenancy.
a. r. p.	£ s. d.	£ s. d.	£ s. d.		£ s. d.
213 0 17	110 5 0	110 0 0	90 0 0		

MEATH.

16 2 20	24 0 0	21 0 0	20 0 0	By mineral.	
3 1 10	8 10 0	9 5 0	7 0 0	do.	
14 2 3	13 10 0	17 2 0	13 10 0		
35 0 16	13 15 0	16 0 0	18 0 0		
3 2 60	3 0 0	2 10 0	2 3 0		
65 1 8	30 0 0	68 17 0	64 13 0		

COUNTY.

25 0 31	21 15 0	33 0 0	17 5 0		
12 1 18	8 15 0	9 0 0	7 7 6		
3 2 0	uncertained,	1 10 0	0 11 6		
69 3 0	uncertained,	39 5 0	24 10 0		
21 3 35	12 0 0	15 9 0	7 17 6		
13 2 8	19 5 0	32 5 0	17 0 0		
8 3 0	5 5 0	6 5 0	6 5 0		
105 1 6	83 0 0	94 19 5	67 10 6		
44 2 8	50 0 0	57 14 0	18 0 0		
183 1 7	180 10 0	190 16 10	135 10 0		
20 1 0	10 15 0	16 14 6	15 5 0		
11 3 12	5 15 0	6 18 0	5 5 0		
14 0 0	4 10 0	4 12 5	4 13 6		
0 3 34	4 0 0	5 0 0	4 8 0		
32 1 23	8 10 0	13 3 6	13 10 0		
11 1 0	11 10 0	15 0 0	7 0 0		
2 1 28	2 0 0	3 4 3	1 10 0		

QUEEN'S

Names of Assistant Commissioners by whom Cases were decided.	No.	Name of Tenant.	Name of Landlord.	Townland.
Assistant Commissioners—				
L. Doyle (Legal). J. MacKenzie. J. Patterson.	1815	Catherine Winlaw, Ltd. Admin. of Martin Whelan.	Lord Castletown, ...	Knockardgannon,
	1816	Martin Hennessy, ...	do.	Ballagh,
	1816	G. & Son, ...	R. McDonnell, Mary Farley, and others.	Burrow,
	1817	John Keenan, ...	Rev. William N. Ouimcan, ...	Ballyroan,
	1818	Richard Williams, ...	George S. Perry, ...	Maidenwoney,
	1819	John Fitzgerald, senr.	R. A. Byron, Batris, of Mrs. M. T. Egan.	Ballyboggy,
	1820	Michael Peters, ...	do.	do.
	1821	William Delany, ...	Sir K. D. Borrowes, ...	Derrykearn,
	1822	Mary Clear, ...	Miss A. F. Owen, ...	Gerrybeg,
	1823	Elizabeth Clooney, ...	do.	do.
	1824	Margaret Moore, ...	Mrs. K. D. King-Harman, ...	Coolbarry,
	1825	Jeremiah Phelan, ...	Lord Garbarry, ...	Parkmahoyvy,
	1826	Timothy Delany, ...	The Commissioners of Endowed Schools.	Clopard,
	1827	John and Anne Dowling,	do.	Cappaloughlin,
	1828	Laughlin Laughlin, ...	Richard Caldbeck,	Killeshenley,
	1829	Do. ...	Major-General Hayman, ...	do.
	1830	Patrick Nolan, ...	H. F. Palmer, ...	Kuackdall,
	1831	James Shearan, ...	do.	do.
	1832	Andrew Curris, ...	O. A. Perat, ...	Mount Oliver and another.
	1833	Do. ...	do.	Derrakillsallegarsin Uarnay.
	1834	John Feehan, Esq. at M. Feehan.	Rev. W. Lywler, in pursuance of C. J. Lywler, a minor, by N. Lywler, his mother and their children, and John Gordon.	Kanaturor,
	1835	Michael Phelan, ...	Mrs. Frances Owens, ...	Currin in Ossory,
				Total,

COUNTY OF

Assistant Commissioners—	2201	Myles Doyle, Limited Administrator of Michael Doyle.	Colonel John G. Hone & ors.,	Toumtaniboy,
R. R. Kane (Legal). L. Crosby.				
R. R. Kane (Legal). M. F. Lynch. L. Crosby.	2202	Martin Flood, ...	Lord Carew, ...	Ballyland
	2203	Thomas Kavanagh, ...	G. W. G. Barry, ...	Bartanna,
	2204	Margaret Whelan, ...	Earl of Portsmouth, continued in name of the Right Hon. Newton, Earl of Portsmouth.	Ornan,

COUNTY—*continued.*

Extent of Holding Acres.	Poor Law Valuation.	Former Rent.	Judicial Rent.	Observations.	Value of Tenancy.
A. R. P.	£ s. d.	£ s. d.	£ s. d.		£ s. d.
18 3 16	unascertained	6 10 0	4 7 8		
3 0 10	3 10 0	3 13 4	8 12 6		
19 1 13	23 10 0	38 0 0	29 10 0		
3 1 29	3 15 0	6 10 0	8 5 0		
3 1 32	8 10 0	6 16 11	6 16 11		
13 2 13	9 5 0	27 3 0	16 10 0		
9 2 83	3 10 0	4 16 0	3 0 0		
120 2 2	64 0 0	80 0 0	62 5 0		
1 1 0	—	1 10 0	0 16 0		
7 1 3	4 5 0	4 0 0	3 7 6		
3 3 36	3 0 0	6 0 0	3 0 0		
44 2 0	18 10 0	32 0 0	17 5 0		
36 0 0	18 15 0	23 15 0	16 10 0		
23 0 20	13 0 0	19 11 6	16 10 0		
46 0 26	29 0 0	33 0 0	27 10 0		
34 3 13	23 0 0	81 0 0	18 10 0		
8 3 3	7 0 0	13 16 0	9 5 0		
3 1 30	2 15 0	5 0 0	3 17 6		
100 0 0	91 10 0	108 16 0	64 0 0		
62 8 0	45 0 0	37 13 10	31 0 0		
11 3 36	9 15 0	16 0 0	7 10 0		
3 0 36	5 5 0	6 10 0	5 10 0		
1,339 3 33	704 5 0	900 1 8	716 11 11		

Names of Assistant Commissioners by whom Cases were decided.	No.	Name of Tenant.	Name of Landlord.	Townland.
Assistant Commissioners—				
R. B. Kane (Legal). M. P. Lynch. L. Carney.	3305	Thomas Geoghegan,	Earl of Portsmouth, mentioned in name of the Right Hon. Newton, Earl of Portsmouth.	Cranerkilagh,
	3306	John Murphy,	do.	do.
	3307	John Ennis,	do.	Gortally,
	3308	Mary Murphy,	Sir John T. Power, Bart.,	Kilmew,
	3309	Patrick Murphy,	do.	Ballyvoolock,
	3310	John Harrington,	Captain W. M. Westropp Dawson	Ballyanco,
	3311	Myles Corin,	Patrick Keating,	Monrylore,
	3312	Thomas Mullet,	Rev. F. V. Thornton,	Rathmore,
	3313	Bridget Nolan,	do.	do.
	3314	Martin Newton,	Mrs. A. Bolton and another,	Moharry,
	3315	Charles Kelly,	W. G. Thomas,	Tonmoyle,
	3316	Francis Cullen,	M. A. Maher,	Kilbride,
	3317	Do.	do.	do.
	3318	Mrs. Johanna Cleary,	E. M. Richards,	Ardkira Fitz, Upper,
	3319	Thomas Breen,	do.	do.
	3320	Michael Neall (Neill),	do.	do.
	3321	Denis Coppoert,	Mrs. J. L. Commden,	Rathdall,
	3322	Myles O'Brien,	John H. Talbot,	Dallinglough,
	3323	Edward Boyer,	John Doxworth,	Ballybrogagh,
	3324	Samuel Bowman,	Hunter Callan,	Knowerry,
	3325	Michael Lennon,	James Hewetin,	Dangern,
	3326	Anne and Peter Shortall,	A. de P. O'Kelly, contd. in name of John P. O'Kelly & ors.	Ballyhoggan, Lr.,
	3327	John Voley,	Miss D. Sparrow and others,	Ardaugh, Little,
	3328	Thomas Eliot,	Sir John T. Power, Bart.,	Thurtomorvile,
				Total,

Assistant Commissioners—				
R. B. Kane (Legal). P. Gallan. C. B. Butler.	6330	Thomas Fallon,	James Davis,	Clanahan Davis,
	6331	Winifred Hogan,	Trustees of C. N. Bagot,	Holygrove,
	6332	John Conboy,	do.	Ballyhlark,

WEXFORD—*continued.*

Extent of Holdings in Statute.	Poor Law Valuation.	Former Rent.	Judicial Rent.	Observations.	Value of Tenancy.
A. R. P.	£ s. d.	£ s. d.	£ s. d.		£ s. d.
40 3 28	26 0 0	25 3 0	25 3 6		
54 3 15	36 10 0	40 16 0	33 0 0		
4 0 0	0 10 0	2 0 0	0 15 0		
15 3 30	unascertained,	11 6 3	10 5 0		
13 1 18	8 0 0	9 3 10	7 10 0		
5 3 3	unascertained,	3 3 4	2 2 0		
34 1 0	14 16 0	16 3 0	13 10 0		
57 3 2	23 15 0	25 0 0	21 0 0		
4 3 5	2 15 0	3 4 0	1 10 0		
18 1 30	5 15 0	6 16 0	5 0 0		
23 0 16	6 0 0	11 0 0	8 8 0		
51 3 10	33 0 0	51 1 3	28 12 0		
71 0 0	45 15 0	62 9 9	45 10 0		
68 3 19	24 10 0	30 4 11	27 10 0		
21 3 19	6 0 0	8 4 6	5 10 0		
13 1 16	3 10 0	6 5 6	3 15 0		
57 1 5	11 10 0	19 7 0	12 7 0		
5 3 30	6 10 0	9 10 0	7 7 0		
16 0 16	10 10 0	11 0 0	10 0 0		
121 3 9	62 0 0	124 0 0	76 15 0		
60 1 34	22 0 0	26 10 9	20 0 0		
17 3 16	unascertained,	22 5 0	11 10 0		
57 0 19	23 0 0	37 10 4	29 0 0		
29 0 26	19 0 0	33 16 4	17 17 0		
876 1 33	447 5 0	605 0 6	443 5 6		

CONNAUGHT.

GALWAY.

COUNTY OF

Names of Assistant Commissioners by whom Cases were decided.	No.	Name of Tenant.	Name of Landlord.	Townland.
Assistant Commissioners:—				
R. B. Kane (Legal). F. Gallan. C. R. Bryan.	6933	John Conboy, ...	Trustees of C. N. Regan. ...	Curraghavoghla,
	6934	Bernard Geraghty, ...	do. ...	Curraghavoghla, ...
	6935	Catherine Hogan, ...	do. ...	Knockomurrisy,
	6936	Bernard Geraghty, ...	do. ...	do. ...
	6937	Andrew Martin, ...	do. ...	Drivum, ...
	6938	Lawrence Connolly, ...	do. ...	Sheerumstry, ...
	6939	Bridget Geraghty, ...	do. ...	Easton field, ...
	6940	Michael Flanigan, ...	do. ...	Millmore, ...
	6941	Martin Clarke, ...	Sir Edmund Brudefoyd, Bart.	Drumoads,
	6942	Michael Conlon, ...	do. ...	do. ...
	6943	Thomas Craven, ...	do. ...	do. ...
	6944	Michael Conlon "(Lake)"	do. ...	do. ...
	6945	John Foley, ...	do. ...	do. ...
	6946	Bridget Graham, ...	do. ...	do. ...
	6947	Catherine Conlon, ...	do. ...	do. ...
	6948	Michael Foley, ...	do. ...	do. ...
	6949	Pat Graven, senior, ...	do. ...	do. ...
	6950	Mat Graven, ...	do. ...	do. ...
	6951	Mary Conyngham, Ltd. Admr. of Marven Flannery.	Trustees of Vincent Westervdle	Cloughloreak and meelhy,
	6952	John Connolly, ...	do. ...	Ballinmorra (Westerville),
	6953	Luke M'Loughlin, ...	do. ...	do. ...
	6954	Michael Hannin, ...	do. ...	do. ...
	6955	John Kinvum, ...	do. ...	do. ...
	6956	Michael Conyngham, ...	John Fallon, constituted in name of Ursula Fallon.	Tammant, ...
	6957	Mary Clarke, ...	do. ...	do. ...
	6958	Lawrence Carty, ...	do. ...	do. ...
	6959	Pat Lohan, ...	do. ...	do. ...
	6960	Patrick Murry, ...	do. ...	do. ...
	6961	Martin Griffin, ...	do. ...	do. ...
	6962	Lawrence Graven, Ltd. Admr. of Luke Graven, deceased.	do. ...	do. ...
	6963	Michael Clarke, ...	do. ...	do. ...
	6964	Thomas Donley, ...	do. ...	do. ...
	6965	Michael Donnin, ...	do. ...	do. ...
	6966	Michael Murkley, ...	do. ...	do. ...

Extent of Holding. Acres.	Poor Law Valuation.	Former Rent.	Judicial Rent.	Observations.	Va
A. R. P.	£ s. d.	£ s. d.	£ s. d.		
10 0 5	5 15 0	5 15 0	5 15 0		
4 2 30	1 10 0	1 9 0	1 4 0		
14 1 0	unascertained,	5 5 0	4 5 0		
12 3 33	do.	4 5 0	4 0 0		
10 0 15	6 0 0	9 5 11	6 5 0		
15 1 30	3 0 0	5 5 5	5 10 0		
3 0 16	1 15 0	2 0 0	1 15 0		
25 0 32	unascertained,	6 9 1	6 0 8		
5 5 25	3 5 0	9 7 0	5 7 0	And 1/4th of 18s. 1s. 14s.	
9 3 6	2 14 6	6 15 6	5 15 0	do.	
11 3 3	6 5 0	6 4 0	5 4 0	do.	
16 5 7	4 16 0	4 15 0	4 15 0	do.	
10 3 23	3 11 0	5 10 0	5 10 0	do.	
7 3 25	3 15 0	2 16 0	2 16 0	do.	
9 0 33	5 13 6	5 11 6	3 6 6	do.	
6 5 4	2 15 0	2 16 0	2 2 0	do.	
12 2 20	6 14 0	3 15 0	5 15 0	do.	
10 1 25	3 8 0	3 7 6	3 5 6	do.	
3 1 7	2 0 0	1 13 6	1 12 8	And 1/5th of the grazing of 1s. 6s. 10s.	
7 1 30	5 15 0	4 0 6	3 13 6		
13 2 23	6 5 0	7 6 6	5 13 0		
11 5 21	5 5 0	5 15 6	6 16 0		
4 1 33	8 0 0	2 6 0	2 6 0		
23 2 16	5 10 0	5 4 6	6 0 0	With right of grazing 6 acres in common with 16 others.	
10 3 36	4 10 0	4 5 10	3 15 0	do.	
7 3 14	2 5 6	2 7 4	2 7 0	do.	
4 5 25	2 5 0	2 16 3	2 6 0	do.	
12 5 23	4 5 0	4 14 6	4 0 0	do.	
5 1 0	6 0 0	1 15 7	1 15 7	do.	
5 0 19	1 10 0	1 15 7	1 15 7	do.	
5 0 17	1 10 0	1 15 7	1 15 7	do.	
6 3 30	2 5 0	2 7 4	2 2 0	do.	
7 0 51	2 5 0	2 13 3	8 4 0	do.	
13 2 0	5 2 0	5 6 6	4 4 0	do.	

COUNTY OF

Names of Assistant Commissioners by whom Cases were decided.	No.	Name of Tenant.	Name of Landlord.	Townland.
Assistant Commissioners— R. R. Kane (Legal), F. Gallar. G. B. Bryers.	5967	Pat. Buffery,	John Fallon, consid. in name of Charles Fallon.	Townurd,
	5968	Michael Ellis,	do.	do.
	5969	James Henry,	do.	do.
	5970	Pat Mackler,	do.	do.
	5971	Matthew Curry,	do.	do.
				Total,

COUNTY OF

Assistant Commissioners— K. Green (Legal), J. H. McConnell. R. W. Crampton.	1390	Daniel Croaser,	George Marsham,	Kiladivooll and agasalry.
	4391	John McAvveary,	do.	Killoymorlan,
	1392	Denis McCaffrey,	Mrs. A. Perry,	Ardamanta,
	4393	John Stratton,	Mrs. Pritchard Rayner Seton,	Drumbich,
	1391	Patrick McAvveary,	William La Touche,	Derrinkohet Roynardt,
	4395	Patrick Dolan,	Patrick Welsh,	Cranaghnrughmore,
	4396	Anne Meehan, Limited Admit. of Jas Meehan	do.	Kishan Globe,
	4397	Bridget Costello,	do.	Cranaghnrughmore,
	4398	Bridget Common,	do.	do.
	1399	Edward Prion,	William Arms,	Capalan,
	4400	Margaret Brown,	do.	Gargar,
	4401	Patrick Flynn,	do.	Drumara,
	4402	Nora McFerran, Limited Admit. of Jas. McBrien	do.	Glenanlerg,
	4403	Margaret Fox,	do.	Belganard,
				Total,

COUNTY OF

TABLE OF JUDICIAL RENTS.

GALWAY—continued.

Extent of Holding. Statute.	Poor Law Valuation.	Former Rent.	Judicial Rent.	Observations.
A. R. P.	£ s. d.	£ s. d.	£ s. d.	
3 0 4	1 18 0	1 18 7	1 15 7	With right of grazing 8 turns with 16 others.
16 0 22	5 0 6	5 6 7	4 12 6	do.
8 3 23	1 10 0	2 19 5	3 13 3	do.
10 2 26	2 15 6	5 2 10	3 6 0	do.
5 3 35	3 0 0	1 15 7	1 15 6	do.
110 3 1	143 10 0	164 19 8	130 2 8	

LEITRIM.

1 3 20	1 11 0	3 5 0	2 6 0	
20 0 13	10 10 0	6 0 0	8 0 0	
9 1 0	5 5 0	5 0 0	4 0 0	By consent.
6 2 9	4 10 0	4 5 6	3 17 0	
16 1 21	6 13 0	6 7 0	7 0 0	
11 3 0	6 0 0	7 10 0	6 0 0	
7 2 23	3 0 0	6 16 0	3 14 0	
13 0 13	7 0 0	7 3 6	6 5 0	
6 1 20	5 5 0	5 15 0	4 0 0	
22 3 17	13 15 0	16 0 0	13 15 0	
19 1 13	10 10 0	6 10 0	8 16 0	
30 3 38	15 0 0	20 0 0	10 10 0	
14 0 0	8 19 0	9 10 0	6 0 0	
13 2 30	7 5 0	8 10 0	6 18 0	
313 3 10	105 4 0	115 13 6	87 3 0	

ROSCOMMON.

COUNTY OF

Names of Assistant Commissioners by whom Cases were decided.	No.	Name of Tenant.	Name of Landlord.	Townland.
Assistant Commissioners— W. F. BAKER (Legal). T. MAGAFEL. L. W. BYRNE.	6749	Patrick Mulvannan,	R. F. Worthington,	Limerypad,
	6751	Ellen Grady,	do.	do.
	6752	John Lowry,	do.	do.
	6743	Thomas McDonagh,	do.	do.
	6744	John Lowry (Andrew),	do.	do.
	6745	Francis Dowd,	do.	do.
	6746	John Redington,	Patrick M. Leonard,	Cloonfinnoway,
	6747	John Prendergast,	do.	do.
	6748	Thomas Fleming,	Mrs. C. G. Magrath, contd. in name of Miss A. L. D. Magrath.	Adrumad
	6749	Pat Griffin,	Patrick M. Leonard,	Cloonfinnoway,
	6750	Martin Jennings,	do.	do.
	6751	John Byrne,	do.	do.
	6752	Pat Prendergast,	do.	do.
	6753	Thomas Higgins,	do.	do.
	6754	John Gannon,	do.	do.
	6755	Thomas Gannon,	do.	do.
	6756	Mary McManus,	Mrs. F. D. Chambers,	Chambyberry,
	6757	John Judge,	James Coyne,	Clogawvin,
	6758	Michael Mannion and another.	Robert F. T. Logan,	Cloonfad, East.
	6759	John Nevon,	Reginald K. Knox and others,	Cookson,
	6760	James Fleming	Abraham Logan contained in name of R. F. T. Logan.	Cloonfad,
	6761	Stephen Bannan,	do.	do.
	6762	Anne Fleming,	do.	do.
	6763	Frank Brannon,	do.	do.
	6764	James Jennings,	do.	do.
	6765	James Kerrigan,	do.	do.
	6766	Pat Quinn,	do.	do.
	6767	Anthony Mullin,	do.	do.
	6768	Peter Rogers,	do.	do.

ROSCOMMON—*continued.*

Extent of Holding. Acres.	Poor Law Valuation	Former Rent.	Judicial Rent.	Observations	Value of Tenancy
A. R. P.	£ s. d.	£ s. d.	£ s. d.		£ s. d.
5 0 0	4 0 0	4 5 0	3 16 0		
5 0 14	1 0 0	3 2 6	1 0 0		
6 2 23	5 0 0	6 15 7	0 5 0		
11 1 3	6 5 0	5 10 0	8 0 0		
15 3 4	8 5 0	0 2 0	5 18 0		
10 0 0	2 15 0	3 12 6	2 10 0		
3 0 18	1 0 0	1 16 0	1 4 0		
11 1 14	5 0 0	5 7 0	5 0 0		
18 3 30	2 15 0	8 0 0	4 4 0		
4 1 37	3 12 0	3 0 0	1 15 0		
6 1 37	2 10 0	3 17 6	1 16 0		
11 1 14	1 10 0	5 12 4	3 0 0		
11 1 14	6 15 0	5 7 0	3 0 0		
22 2 29	8 5 0	6 4 0	6 0 0		
18 0 36	7 5 0	7 13 0	4 10 0		
18 0 36	7 5 0	7 15 0	6 0 0		
4 2 20	4 0 0	3 16 10	2 10 0		
15 1 30	13 15 0	15 15 0	11 0 0		
11 3 7	5 10 0	5 10 0	6 15 0		
22 5 28	2 0 0	9 0 0	5 10 6		
14 1 18	3 5 0	3 11 6	3 5 0		
28 1 17	13 10 0	8 5 0	7 0 0		
12 2 13	5 15 0	6 0 0	4 4 0		
14 0 9	3 5 0	5 11 6	2 15 0		
18 5 34	3 10 0	3 11 8	3 5 0		
16 3 21	5 5 0	7 0 0	1 5 0		
15 3 34	6 15 0	6 10 0	6 0 0		
18 3 23	3 15 0	3 18 0	2 18 0		
18 2 18	0 10 0	8 0 0	6 10 0		
532 1 31	189 10 0	199 17 7	189 17 0		

PROVINCE OF

COUNTY OF

Name of Assistant Commissioners by whom Cases were decided.	No.	Name of Tenant.	Name of Landlord.	Townland.
Assistant Commissioners—				
L. Dyer (Legal), W. Walpole, C. O'Keeffe.	3632	Patrick Darby, ...	Mrs. Anne Reed, ...	Rawnatroon, ...
	3633	James Prout,	Colonel Jesse Lloyd,	Farranroory,
	3634	Do. —	do. ...	do.
				Total,

CIVIL BILL

PROVINCE OF

COUNTY OF

Name of County Court Judge.	No.	Name of Tenant.	Name of Landlord.	Townland.
Alexander Warren, &c.	1743	Mary A. Mullen,	E. J. Saunderson, ...	Anghagubrick,
	1744	Margaret Brady, ...	Maxwell J. Boyle, ...	Hofrasoon,
	1745	Mark Murtagh,	Robert J. Barrows, ...	Tullyard,
	1746	Michael Mahon, ...	Mrs. Sophia J. Rogers, ...	Drentaroagh,
	1747	Do.	do. —	do.
				Total,

COUNTY OF

MUNSTER.

TIPPERARY.

Extent of Holding, &c.	Poor Law Valuation	Former Rent	Judicial Rent	Observations	Value of Tenancy
A. R. P.	£ s. d.	£ s. d.	£ s. d.		£ s. d.
1 0 24	3 10 0	2 10 0	1 12 6		
63 3 15	unascertained	64 0 0	39 0 0		
11 3 34	do.	11 16 0	7 10 0		
102 0 7	1 10 0	78 4 0	43 3 6		

COURTS.

ULSTER.

CAVAN.

Nature of Holding, &c.	Poor Law Valuation	Former Rent	Judicial Rent	Observations	Term of Tenancy
A. R. P.	£ s. d.	£ s. d.	£ s. d.		£ s. d.
11 0 10	9 0 0	10 12 0	9 0 0		
6 0 0	—	5 0 0	7 0 0		
28 0 35	18 0 0	17 10 6	15 10 0		
7 3 5	5 8 0	6 10 0	4 10 0		
8 3 73	5 0 0	8 0 0	4 10 0		
60 1 33	37 8 0	47 12 6	33 10 0		

DONEGAL.

PROVINCE OF

KINGS

County Court Judge.	No.	Name of Tenant.	Name of Landlord.	Townland.
J. A. Curran, q.c.	228	John Smith ...	James H. Patrickson,	Okenbeme,
	229	Anne Poland,	William W. Marshall,	Ballindrenan,
	230	Mathew Flanagan,	William H. Gardiner & ors.,	Aughavullah,
	231	Patrick Dunne	Captain Thomas A. Drought,	Ballinamerig,
	232	Anne Poland,	do.	do.
	233	John Wyher,	do.	do.
				Total,

COUNTY OF

J. A. Curran, q.c.	302	John Dowd,	Patrick Dowd,	Dungan,
	303	Patrick Byrne,	Patrick Kennedy,	Towlagh,
	304	Sylvester Reilly,	Anne Luby,	Hatherahrick,
				Total,

PROVINCE OF

COUNTY OF

LEINSTER.

COUNTY.

Extent of Holding, Statute.	Poor Law Valuation.	Former Rent.	Judicial Rent.	Observations.	Value of Tenancy.
A. R. P.	£ s. d.	£ s. d.	£ s. d.		£ s. d.
27 3 19	10 5 0	7 0 0	7 3 0	By consent.	
15 2 5	9 0 0	6 10 0	6 15 0		
53 2 34	13 0 0	11 0 0	11 0 0		
16 0 31	11 15 0	10 0 0	7 10 0		
22 0 25	19 0 0	19 3 10	16 15 0		
124 2 36	72 15 0	100 0 0	78 0 0		
243 0 30	141 15 0	154 13 10	131 3 0		

MEATH.

8 1 36	unascertained.	4 0 0	3 11 0		
16 1 22	13 0 0	13 13 0	13 5 0		
13 0 0	10 0 0	17 13 0	8 10 0		
37 3 15	23 0 0	33 6 0	25 6 0		

CONNAUGHT.

MAYO.

LAND LAW (IRELAND) ACT, 1887.

LEASEHOLDERS.

PROVINCE OF

COUNTY OF

Names of Assistant Commissioners by whom Cases were decided.	No.	Name of Tenant.	Name of Landlord.	Townland.
Assistant Commissioners— H. Green (Legal). H. Jellicoe. A. R. Montgomery.	1545	James Lowery, ...	John Wardlow, ...	Claughrey, ...
	1566	David Rea, ...	John Armstrong, ...	Crunhill, ...
	1567	Patrick McNeill, ...	Mary McNeill and another, Reps. of Rosetta Harrison,	Growhill, ...
	1568	Archibald Johnston, ...	do.	do. ...
	1569	John Warrick, ...	do.	do. ...
	1570	George Jamieson, ...	Lord O'Neill, ...	Revakagh, ...
	1571	Andrew McDermott, ...	John B. Dunlop, ...	Mana, ...
				Total, ...

COUNTY OF

Assistant Commissioners— W. F. Bailey (Legal). T. A. Dillon. T. Davidson.	337	Thomas Beatty, ...	Mrs. Elizabeth Swaney, ...	Mullynagowan,...
	338	Patrick Fee, ...	George Massey Beresford, ...	Garthmoehien, ...
	339	James C. Moore and ors.,	The Earl of Erne, ...	Carraghroe ...
	340	William Moore, ...	do.	Moneyreakin, ...
				Total, —

PROVINCE OF

COUNTY OF

Re-m Commission.	448	John Ryan, ...	Lord Rathdonnell, ...	Tobinstown and residue;
	449	Julia A. Ryan and anor.,	do. ...	do. ...
				Total, ...

ULSTER.

ANTRIM.

Extent of Holding, Acreage.	Poor Law Valuation	Former Rent.	Judicial Rent.	Observations.	Value of Tenancy.
A. R. P.	£ s. d.	£ s. d.	£ s. d.		£ s. d.
40 0 0	33 10 0	27 16 0	21 10 0		
61 0 0	24 5 0	30 0 0	23 0 0		
33 2 23	18 10 0	14 6 0	11 5 0	By consent.	
27 0 13	18 15 0	13 0 0	11 1 0	do.	
32 1 13	16 10 0	17 7 6	14 15 6	do.	
94 0 0	59 13 0	60 0 0	45 0 0		
15 1 31	9 5 0	8 3 6	7 10 0		
305 2 1	163 5 5	190 13 0	157 1 4		

FERMANAGH.

18 0 31	16 18 0	20 0 0	15 0 0		
4 3 21	4 10 0	2 15 6	2 15 6		
141 3 6	92 0 0	85 0 0	70 0 0		
50 0 12	63 0 0	46 0 0	33 0 0		
213 1 36	176 8 0	153 16 6	123 16 6		

LEINSTER.

CARLOW.

COUNTY OF

Names of Assistant Commissioners by whom Cases were decided.	No.	Name of Tenant.	Name of Landlord.	Townland.
Assistant Commissioners:—				
D. E. Hays (Legal). J. Haldiston. A. V. Coate.	707	Michael Flanagan,	Michael Keogh,	Walkinstown,
	708	Do.	do.	Overhills & ora.,
	709	Do.	Elizabeth M. Richardson,	Oranlia,
	710	Patrick Mooney,	Mrs. J. F. Hopper,	Stannaway Granelia
	711	Joseph Mooney,	do.	Glasnevy,
	712	James Perry,	Mrs. A. G. M. Verschoyle,	Oranlia,
	713	Rev. T. Fahy and anr.,	Rev. F. D. D. La Touche and another,	Mod Cow,
	714	James James,	Captain G. R. Darley, &c.,	Allagove,
	715	Anne Morren,	Major E. G. Grogan,	Gokicol,
	716	Martin Mahon,	Joseph P. Tyndall,	Kilfinnadan,
				Total,

COUNTY OF

Assistant Commissioners:—	No.	Name of Tenant.	Name of Landlord.	Townland.
L. Doyle (Legal). W. Walpole. G. O'Keeffe,	530	John Lynch,	Rev. William B. Foyen,	Courtmbunkey and others.
	531	Henry C. Gregory, Exor. of Rev. C. D. Servante.	Michael Riordan and others,	Westown & Demesne
	532	Martin Lynch,	Robert Neville and another,	Alnamore,
	533	Bridget Bohan, contd. in name of John Bohan.	do.	Alnamore, South,
	534	Daniel J. Stapleton,	Thomas Ashbrook,	Tullamore,
	535	Michael Lavaryn,	William King,	Brown,
	536	Michael MacKay, Admor. of Richard Mackay.	William Robertson,	Monamore,
	537	John Walsh,	Oliver C. Oliver and others,	Mallardstown, Lr. and another.
L. Doyle (Legal). E. R. Davey. R. Garland.	538	Anne Jullien, Rep. of Thomas Jullien.	Earl of Chamel,	Castleverhick,
	539	John Holohan,	James Howlett,	Castlecabob,
	540	James Ryan,	Mrs. Elisa Dogny,	Whitfield,
	541	Jessie Treacy,	Mary Webb, Rep. of George O. Webb.	Caim,
	542	John Phelan,	H. W. M'Creary,	New Park,
	543	John Prendergast,	Vincent Childe,	Church Hill,
	544	John Hogan,	Nicholas P. O'Shea,	Wallslough,
	545	Thomas Madigan,	Anne J. Ambrose,	Kilbriagh & anor.,
				Total,

DUBLIN.

Extent of Holding. Statute	Poor Law Valuation.	Former Rent.	Judicial Rent.	Observations.	Value of Tenancy.
A. R. P.	£ s. d.	£ s. d.	£ s. d.		£ s. d.
2 0 0	6 0 0	10 5 11	7 0 0		
37 3 01	65 15 0	90 11 3	66 0 0		
2 3 10	unascertained,	16 0 0	11 5 0		
39 0 39	60 0 0	103 5 5	50 0 0		
10 0 0	50 0 0	82 13 6	70 0 0		
31 1 16	68 0 0	125 0 0	67 0 0		
29 3 6	32 0 0	46 6 0	40 0 0		
11 1 16	9 10 0	11 3 8	6 16 0		
83 6 13	60 0 0	113 14 3	73 0 0		
16 3 15	10 0 0	30 5 10	50 0 0		
807 0 28	370 5 0	635 1 7	478 0 0		

KILKENNY.

127 0 4	62 15 0	70 0 0	60 0 0		
15 1 30	26 0 0	60 0 0	50 0 0		
187 0 0	unascertained,	100 0 0	85 0 0		
166 3 15	73 0 0	63 10 0	66 0 0		
610 1 34	300 0 0	540 13 0	226 15 0		
50 0 31	85 3 0	33 0 0	77 3 6		
33 3 6	9 13 0	32 0 0	13 15 0		
85 3 20	28 8 0	59 0 0	35 7 0		
83 1 31	73 0 0	60 3 4	81 0 0		
103 0 6	80 5 0	76 0 0	62 15 0		
104 3 16	67 14 0	73 3 6	18 0 0		
138 3 6	85 15 0	64 0 0	46 0 0		
0 0 7	2 10 0	3 0 0	6 10 0		
22 1 7	16 16 0	21 0 0	15 13 8		
68 0 0	41 0 0	49 13 1	30 10 0		

Names of Assistant Commissioners by whom Cases were decided.	No.	Name of Tenant.	Name of Landlord.	Townland
Assistant Commissioners—				
W. P. Bailey (Legal).	754	John Connell,	Mr. Henry P. De Bath.	Knightstown,
S. Byrne.	755	William Brady,	do.	do.
C. W. Thorpe.	756	Catherine Carpenter,	do.	do.
	757	Laurence Monaghan,	do.	Ladytalk,
	758	Thomas Donegan,	do.	do.
	759	Patrick McGahan,	do.	do.
	760	Thomas Reilly,	do.	do.
	761	John Traynor,	do.	do.
	762	Owen Henay, senior,	do.	do.
	763	John Traynor,	do.	do.
	764	Owen Henay, junior,	do.	do.
	765	James Flanagan,	do.	do.
	766	Patrick Owens,	do.	do.
	767	William Talgan,	do.	do.
	768	James Hughes,	do.	do.
	769	Michael McDaniel,	do.	do.
	770	Eliza Hardie,	do.	do.
	771	Matthew Ryan,	do.	Knightstown,
	772	Michael Reilly,	do.	do.
	773	Anne Carpenter,	do.	do.
	774	Richard McKeon,	do.	do.
	775	Thomas Caskey,	do.	do.
	776	Thomas Martin,	Thomas Garrard,	Oldro Cloughil,
	777	Do.	do.	Cloughil,
	778	Matthew Mullan,	Fitzhenry Smith,	Ardrumichan,
				Total,

Assistant Commissioners—	106	Robert Perry and Son, Limited.	Robert Gun Brady,	Rathdowney,
L. Doyle (Legal).	107	Mary McEvoy,	Rev. R. Fitzgerald,	Oraigneanbowen,
J. MacKenzie.	110	Thomas Roe,	Sir Charles Coote, Bart.,	Bumhall
C. W. Thorpe.				

MEATH.

Extent of Holding. Acreage.	Poor Law Valuation.	Former Rent.	Judicial Rent.	Observations.	Value of Tenancy.
A. R. P.	£ s. d.	£ s. d.	£ s. d.		£ s. d.
8 3 33	3 5 0	5 5 5	4 10 0		
9 1 6	4 5 0	7 0 6	3 5 6		
9 0 37	4 5 0	7 10 0	3 7 4		
3 1 20	3 0 0	3 10 0	1 13 4		
6 1 9	1 10 0	3 0 0	1 10 0		
7 6 60	4 0 0	5 5 0	3 0 0		
4 1 3	3 0 0	4 0 0	3 17 6		
5 3 5	6 0 0	3 15 0	3 13 6		
9 3 20	6 5 0	3 0 0	5 0 0		
3 3 17	unascertained.	3 6 0	1 5 0		
9 1 10	4 15 0	7 15 0	4 4 0		
4 0 29	4 15 0	6 0 0	3 10 0		
7 1 6	6 0 0	6 0 0	4 10 0		
13 0 14	5 0 0	6 5 0	6 10 0		
17 6 60	11 10 0	17 13 0	13 5 0		
19 3 6	13 0 0	13 0 0	9 10 0		
47 0 37	43 0 0	45 0 0	33 13 0		
3 3 29	3 18 0	6 10 0	3 0 0		
1 3 14½	4 0 0	1 0 0	0 17 3		
0 3 17	unascertained.	0 11 5	0 19 0		
5 0 0	1 15 0	3 10 8	1 10 0		
7 3 31	unascertained.	5 10 0	3 10 0		
17 6 17	30 0 0	35 0 0	33 0 0		
340 3 35	330 10 0	533 5 0	330 0 0		
66 6 29	61 0 0	43 15 0	50 0 0		
619 3 25½	636 10 0	637 2 0	576 5 6		

COUNTY.

46 3 17	83 10 0	108 11 3	73 10 0	And right of wandering on &c. &c.	
104 3 37	88 15 0	80 11 11	40 5 0		
133 1 9	131 10 0	130 0 0	108 5 0		

QUEEN'S

Name of Assistant Commissioners by whom cases were decided.	No.	Name of Tenant.	Name of Landlord.	Townland.
Assistant Commissioners—				
L. Doyle (Legal).	611	Patrick Doolan, —	E. Rossetta & ors., Executors of J. W. R. Scott.	Killeany, ...
J. MacEnerth.	612	Henry Lalor, continued in name of Jos. Mole & anor.	Charlotte Mullin, —	Curraragh, ...
J. Patterson.	613	James Sheeran, —	Elizabeth Palmer, —	Ballybeggy, ...
	614	Michael Power, —	R. A. Byrne, Exor. of Mrs. M. T. Egan.	do. ...
	615	Richard Baldwin, Rep. of M. Baldwin.	W. M. Lawrenson, conhd. in the name of Mrs. A. L. J. Lawrenson	Rahawa, —
	616	John M. Clear, —	Mrs A. F. Owens, ...	Garrybeha, —
	617	John Bergin, —	do. ...	do. —
	618	Mary Davis, —	Rev. J. H. Wareford, ...	Clarranassconnly, —
	619	Robert Stanley, —	F. G. Deverell and others, ...	Killoununahlin, ...
	620	Thomas Fletcher, ...	Peter R. White, ... —	do. —
	621	George Bromfield, —	L. T. Rea, —	Harristown, ...
				Total, ...

COUNTY OF

Name of Assistant Commissioners—	No.	Name of Tenant.	Name of Landlord.	Townland.
Assistant Commissioners—				
R. R. Kane (Legal).	1023	John Bevington, —	Captain W. M. W. Dawson,	Ballyoogan, ...
M. P. Lynch.	1024	Joshua Bunk, ...	Col. Robert M. Ireland, ...	Cloham, —
L. Creery.	1025	Garrett Murphy, senior,	do. ...	Davidstown, —
	1026	Andrew Power, —	Charles Morrison, & another, ...	Ballyruhook, ...
	1027	Nicholas Murphy, & anor.	Patrick McGill, —	Kilnew, —
	1028	James Moffett, ...	Lord Carew, —	Knockmore and anor.
	1029	Peter Carty, —	General Solomon Richards, ...	Ballystarthen, —
	1030	Nicholas Murphy, ...	Sir John T. Power, Bart.,	Kilnew, —
	1031	Henry Watkins, ...	Earl of Portsmouth, ...	Oularturd, ...
	1032	do. —	do. —	do. —
	1033	Pierce Lett, ... —	do. —	TomanEagh, ...
	1034	Bernard Bolger, ...	do. —	Killernagan, ...
	1035	Patrick Fortune, ...	do. —	do. —
	1036	Mrs. Elizabeth P. Davis,	do. —	Killinhey, ...
	1037	John Ennis, ...	do. ...	Curhally, ...
	1038	Henry Watkins & anor.	do. ...	Ballinsheerery, ...
	1039	John Doolan, —	do. ...	Kilmacowslow, —

COUNTY—*continued.*

Extent of Holding.	Poor Law Valuation.	Former Rent.	Judicial Rent.	Observations.
a. r. p.	£ s. d.	£ s. d.	£ s. d.	
34 2 0	ascertained.	20 0 0	18 10 0	
67 0 8	64 0 0	51 0 0	85 0 0	
18 3 0	7 13 0	10 18 5	7 8 0	
12 0 6	8 15 0	10 6 0	8 10 0	
5 2 13	1 10 0	3 0 0	1 5 0	
8 1 7	8 15 0	5 0 0	4 10 0	
10 2 6	7 0 0	6 0 0	5 6 1	
85 8 24	73 0 0	69 0 0	78 0 0	
70 0 10	59 10 0	50 10 0	60 0 0	
11 3 3	5 10 0	8 0 0	8 15 0	
45 2 27	35 0 0	37 11 3	65 3 6	
757 1 5	173 10 0	653 17 6	488 6 7	

WEXFORD.

182 5 20	ascertained.	55 13 0	44 13 0	
45 0 25	27 10 0	20 7 6	26 15 0	
70 1 35	18 10 0	16 1 3	9 10 6	
13 1 56	13 10 0	16 10 6	17 10 0	
6 1 24	6 0 0	5 0 0	4 10 6	
63 1 21	54 6 0	65 3 0	39 10 0	
46 2 16	27 10 0	37 10 0	22 0 0	
17 1 7	ascertained.	12 14 6	10 0 0	
75 1 5	64 0 0	56 10 0	47 0 0	
101 1 15	69 0 0	67 15 1	80 0 0	
46 0 83	73 10 0	25 0 0	30 0 0	
87 0 4	25 10 0	50 7 0	28 15 0	
88 1 50	31 6 0	27 5 5	18 18 0	
175 2 16	155 10 0	137 0 0	150 0 0	
88 0 15	55 10 0	54 18 0	54 18 0	
40 1 75	21 0 0	85 6 0	25 0 0	
95 0 50	70 0 0	75 0 0	55 0 0	

IRISH LAND COMMISSION.

Name of Assistant Commissioners by whom Cases were decided.	No.	Name of Tenant.	Name of Landlord.	Townland.
Assistant Commissioners — R. R. KANE (Legal), M. P. LYNCH, L. GRANT.	1040	James Brown, ...	M. K. Prentous,... ...	Ballinsloy, Lower,
	1041	Peter Tobin, ...	Mrs. A. Bolton and another,	Mahoury, ...
	1042	Bryan Murphy, ...	William Wybrants, surviving Trustee of Olivia A. Bolton.	Middletown, ...
	1043	Arthur Murphy, contd. in name of James Murphy,	do.	Middletown and another.
	1044	Philip Warren, ...	William T. Fayle, ...	Cloolealum, ...
	1045	George Dixon, ...	William M. Gildea, ...	Aokabeg, ...
	1046	Catherine Sanborn, ...	Peter Quinary, ...	Moohaugh (title.
	1047	John Carty, ...	Thomas A. Keogh and another, contd. in name of Mary Keogh.	Crossran, ...
	1048	Maria Chapman, ...	John T. Townsham, ...	Ballybough, ...
	1049	Anne Shortall and anor.,	Peathbery de P. O'Kelly, contd. in nature of John M. O'Kelly and another.	Ballyleggan, Lr.,
				Total, ...

WEXFORD—continued.

Extent of Holding. Statute.	Poor Law Valuation.	Former Rent.	Judicial Rent.	Observations.	Value of Tenancy.
A. R. P.	£ s. d.	£ s. d.	£ s. d.		£ s. d.
7 1 16	1 0 0	4 15 0	4 0 0		
55 3 37	48 0 0	41 0 4	34 0 0		
70 1 30	44 15 0	34 0 0	33 0 0		
73 0 14	44 6 0	45 0 0	34 0 0		
43 0 3	31 0 0	27 17 0	33 15 0		
37 1 0	25 0 0	30 0 0	24 3 0		
1 3 19	1 10 0	1 10 0	0 15 0		
64 1 15	31 0 0	60 0 0	63 15 0		
43 1 7	16 10 0	36 0 0	30 0 0		
63 3 21	unascertained.	37 17 3	73 0 0		
1,536 3 21	535 8 0	1,138 15 1	835 17 0		

CONNAUGHT.

GALWAY.

14 1 30	6 10 0	6 0 0	6 0 0		
17 3 10	7 10 0	7 0 0	6 5 0		
33 1 0	14 0 0	13 10 0	13 15 0		

ROSCOMMON.

PROVINCE OF

COUNTY OF

Name of Assistant Commissioner by whom Case was decided.	No.	Name of Tenant.	Name of Landlord.	Townland.
Assistant Commissioners— L. Doyle (Legal), W. Walpole.	226	Richard Bourke,	Count A. J. Moore,	Rosenkiel M,
	227	Jeremiah O'Brien,	Captain G. E. S. M. Dawson,	Glengarriff bridge,
				Total,

CIVIL BILL

PROVINCE OF

COUNTY OF

County Court Judge.	No.	Name of Tenant.	Name of Landlord.	Townland.
George Waters, Q.C.	226	Patrick Reilly,	Earl of Lanesborough,	Drumcryan,
	227	Anne Markey,	Isabella Smith and others,	Tashaw,
	228	Bridget Llittle,	Robert J. Barrows,	Drumbane,
	229	James Curtis,	do.	Drumpurrat,
	230	Patrick Reilly,	do.	Thrugeln,
	231	James Cullen,	Lieut.-Colonel William G. Lloyd and others,	Killrusne,
	232	Patrick Tully,	Edward J. Saunderson,	Cloonal,
	233	Owen Reilly,	do.	Aghadrowagh,
	234	Ross Reilly,	do.	Drumcosh,
	235	Anne Brady,	do.	Drumoghra,
	236	Patrick Smith,	Robert J. Barrows,	Currovegay,
				Total,

COUNTY OF

MUNSTER.

TIPPERARY.

Name of Holding, Acres.	Poor Law Valuation.	Former Rent.	Judicial Rent.	Observations.	Value of Tenancy
A. R. P.	£ s. d	£ s. d.	£ s. d.		£ s. d.
45 3 0	36 0 0	34 16 10	31 0 0	By consent	
38 0 0	12 0 0	13 0 0	12 0 0	do.	
83 3 0	48 0 0	47 16 10	43 0 0		

COURTS.

ULSTER.

CAVAN.

Name of Holding, Acres.	Poor Law Valuation.	Former Rent.	Judicial Rent.	Observations.	Value of Tenancy
A. R. P.	£ s. d	£ s. d.	£ s. d.		£ s. d.
13 1 6	7 10 0	6 5 0	8 0 0		
9 3 9	5 5 0	7 4 6	8 0 0		
20 3 27	14 0 0	11 6 6	9 10 0		
16 3 0	7 0 0	8 6 0	5 10 0		
13 0 16	14 15 0	11 18 1	9 0 0		
16 3 25	9 15 0	11 15 0	8 10 0		
7 1 30	5 0 0	4 16 4	3 18 0		
16 1 11	7 10 0	7 17 6	6 18 6		
33 0 14	10 10 0	10 3 10	8 10 0		
3 0 23	4 0 0	3 13 0	3 0 0		
6 0 13	6 10 0	6 6 0	5 0 0		
143 7 20	91 15 0	89 6 7	70 10 0		

DONEGAL.

PROVINCE OF

COUNTY OF

Clerk of Court Judge	No.	Name of Tenant.	Name of Landlord.	Townland.
J. H. Richardson.	56	William Garrett, ...	Thomas F. Higgins, ...	Clonmacgreen, ...

PROVINCE OF

CONNAUGHT.

MAYO.

Extent of Holding, Acres.	Poor Law Valuation	Former Rent	Judicial Rent	Observations
A. R. P.	£ s. d.	£ s. d.	£ s. d.	
4 3 17	uncertained	3 0 0	3 0 0	

MUNSTER.

CORK.